# THE GREYHOUND
## Breeding, Coursing, Racing, etc.

THE "ASCOT" OF GREYHOUND RACING.

Wembley Stadium, the world's Premier Greyhound Race Track, before a meeting. Nearly 1,000,000 candle power of lighting is used in the Stadium during racing.

# THE
# GREYHOUND

### Breeding, Coursing, Racing, etc.

by
## JAMES
## MATHESON

*Profusely Illustrated*

**HURST & BLACKETT, LTD.**
**PATERNOSTER HOUSE, E.C.**

PRINTED IN GREAT BRITAIN
AT THE ANCHOR PRESS, TIPTREE ,ESSEX

# CONTENTS

# THE GREYHOUND

## Breeding, Coursing, Racing, etc.

### CHAPTER I

#### ORIGIN AND HISTORY OF GREYHOUND RACING

No book concerning greyhounds to-day would be entirely up-to-date without some slight reference to how the sport of greyhound racing was originated and what its development has been.

Everybody who has taken any interest in greyhound racing probably knows that the first attempt at a mechanical hare took place at the Welsh Harp, Hendon, in the year 1876. The apparatus was primitive as compared with the plant now in use, but for that time it was a most ingenious idea, and there is little doubt that had there been organisation in the matter such as we are used to nowadays, improvements would have been made and the sport might have continued and flourished from that time on. It happened, however, that the germ then planted was destined to take life not in this country but on the other side of the Atlantic, in California to be precise. The advance in electricity made it possible for someone with a recollection of the Hendon racing to improve upon it by producing a hare electrically propelled. Even this for a long time was not too satisfactory, but around 1920 mentions of the " Electric Hare " became fairly well known to the readers of " Our Dogs." As the sport progressed in the States, it occurred to Mr. Munn that it was time that it was introduced to the racing-loving people of Great Britain. With this object he made a trip to this country, but it was not so easy as he had thought to bring the new sport into prominence here. Disappointments followed in rapid succession, and it was only when he was on the verge of despair that he happened to interest the one right man—Major Lyne Dixson—to whom is due the subsequent success of greyhound racing. Major Dixson was probably the one man able to handle the situation and overcome the many difficulties, greater even than the difficulty of raising the capital. When he had arranged the detail work which put an end to initial doubts, the money was quickly forthcoming.

Major Lyne Dixson was a coursing judge with a great knowledge of greyhound trainers and greyhounds, both of which were absolutely essential for making a start with racing. Some of the best trainers rallied to the banner of Dixson and in an incredibly short time a track was opened at Manchester, in 1926 exactly fifty years from the date upon which the first attempt at racing greyhounds was made at the Welsh Harp.

At the outset, it was impossible to interest sufficient owners to assure a programme, so the new syndicate (the Greyhound Racing Association) purchased enough

greyhounds of their own—kennelled on the track premises—to guarantee the public a full card on each night
of racing. People gradually became so interested that
many desired to own dogs of their own and, as requests
arrived, the syndicate dogs, one by one at first, and by
scores later, were transferred into private ownership.
Greyhounds from the syndicate were acquired by
personages of the highest standing and title in the land
as well as by tradesmen and artizans. These acquired
dogs, it was arranged, should remain in the Association's
kennels at £1 per week, which sum covered and still
does cover the entire keep and training, no entry fees
being charged. It was imperative that dogs should be
kennelled under the control of the promoters, not
because they wished to exercise any undue influence
or preference in the running of the dogs, but simply
because they had to supervise them in order to guarantee
a full card on each night of racing. Propaganda was
made out of the arrangement, it being stated that the
provision was to keep the sport clean, and so on, but
it is highly probable; had there been any kind of guarantee, enough dogs would always have been available to
fill races if the Association would have added to their
many trials the additional responsibility of looking after
and being responsible for 200 dogs in kennels at one
place. The fact of the dogs being permanently on the
spot achieved one good purpose, that of making it
possible to grade them. No matter what the class

or speed of a particular animal might be, he could be graded into a race which he could win, and during the first season of racing there were very few dogs which did not win in their turn. This was of course to the satisfaction of everybody concerned.

That first season was so successful that the G.R.A. made the necessary arrangements for racing to take place at the White City, London, in the following year. Racing there was carried on in the same way as at Manchester and attracted crowds estimated at up to 100,000 at a single meeting, of which there were three weekly. During the same season the same syndicate opened a track at Harringay to which great crowds went on the three racing nights each week.

The success of greyhound racing being practically assured, companies whose names are now legion quickly came into the field with prospectuses and capital issues, but it remained for the Wembley Stadium and Greyhound Racecourse Co. to come forward with a big comprehensive proposition to purchase the magnificent Stadium at Wembley from the liquidators of the great International Exhibition which had been held at Wembley on two successive years. When the issue of the new Company was launched, it was fully subscribed by half-past nine the same morning; and before the end of the year racing took place at the Stadium. The same system of control with reference to the dogs and their entry in races was adopted as that alluded to above, but it was possible there for outside trainers to bring dogs from elsewhere and run them even if they were not kennelled at the Stadium.

During the second season of greyhound racing very many electric tracks were put into operation in England, Scotland and Ireland, but in a haphazard kind of fashion, and it was in this season that what is now known as " The Trackless Hare " made its appearance.

" The Trackless Hare " is clever in its simplicity and it is claimed for it that it will do all that the electric hare will do. Its devotees are strongly of opinion that the more natural action of the hare makes better racing, but expert opinion is now fairly unanimous in believing that the greyhounds realise quite as vividly as the experts do themselves that the hare is not a thing of life but good enough to race after. At any rate " The Trackless Hare " has its many advantages. It is cheap, and as it requires no mechanical motive power it can be set up in country places where no electricity is available.

In the second season of racing there was a great outcry for a Board of Control for the new sport, as it was felt that the matter was not in the right hands, being left to the promoters, who were financiers only and running the sport for the dividends, their first consideration. Actually, when the White City opened, there was nothing in existence in the shape of a code of rules. Had a serious dispute arisen as to the running of some particular dog in private ownership, there would have been no tribunal to deal with the matter. The G.R.A., wishing reform to come from within and not from without, approached, with the best intentions possible, the National Coursing Club, with a view to getting that old standing body to co-operate in the work of carrying on greyhound racing. This overture on the part of the racing syndicate was attended with complete failure, for the National Coursing Club rightly held that its objects were to see that coursing was carried on in a right and proper manner, and, further, that the sport of coursing had nothing in common with the new sport of greyhound racing, except perhaps that animals of the same breed, even if not of the same breeding, were employed in carrying on both sports. The refusal of the National Coursing Club to associate itself with grey-hound racing was badly received by the promoters at that time, but the N.C.C. had no choice in the matter. With the formation of new companies the calls for a Board of Control became daily more urgent, and many meetings were arranged in the hope that all companies would send representatives and come to some decision as to how best to begin. It remained for the meeting called at Wembley on the inaugural night of that fine company to bring together delegates from all the im-portant flotations, including envoys from the G.R.A., who up until then had declined resolutely to be associ-ated with any of the previous attempts at a full represent-ative meeting for the purpose. The outcome of the

Wembley meeting was the formation of the Grey-hound Club, which will in time, no doubt, accomplish much.

A short history of greyhound racing could not be complete without reference to the petty and badly staged opposition there has been to it on the part of interfering people, whose greatest pain in life is to see others enjoying themselves. No matter how distin-guished these " Kill Joys " may appear to be for the time, we can take it as an absolute fact that they are each and all of them disappointed people in one way or another, out of whom the joy of life has gone, and their one refuge left is to destroy that in others which can never be in themselves. Their first essay was on the G.R.A. on grounds of illegal betting. The G.R.A. allotted positions to a certain number of bookmakers, and to maintain order and facilitate the supervision of these bookmakers the G.R.A. decreed that each book-maker should occupy the same stance on every night of racing, beside a post put up with the man's name. This arrangement, made with the best of intentions, and logical intentions too, as all will agree, was in itself a contravention of a Betting Act. It is a strange thing how much all these reformers know about the works of the devil. *Experientia docet.* The G.R.A. lost their case, of course, but all that happened was that the posts came down and crooked bookmakers were permitted every opportunity of entering the

**B**

premises of the Company and welshing in the crowd. Certain non-party members of the House of Commons were the next to cause a stir. Dreadful representations of the misery and poverty caused by greyhound racing were laid before the Home Secretary but he, unfortunately for the people so interested in others, was compelled to admit that he had no powers to interfere with greyhound racing.

Greyhound racing has been so successful and has caught the desires of the people to such an extent that many vested interests have suffered badly. This is the explanation of so much attempted interference on the part of those who appear to be acting in the best interests of the nation, whereas they are merely the mouthpieces of combines, and others in which they are financially concerned.

Greyhound racing has come to stay. It has come as a health-giving amusement which will undoubtedly do much for the fitness of the people. There has of late years been too much frousting in stuffy halls and places of questionable recreation to the depreciation of the health of the nation, to which the fast falling birth-rate referred to so often of late may perhaps be due.

Betting at greyhound meetings is very small and no bad can come out of money gambled there. A man is as justified in having a shilling on a dog as he is in buying two pints of beer. If he has the one, he cannot have the other, so he has himself to please. The men and women who bet and starve their children are in a very small minority in this country. If they were not, would this country be what it has been and is? Certainly not. There is a great future for the sport, and although it will be run on different lines it is going to remain.

## CHAPTER II

### FUTURE OF THE GREYHOUND

UNTIL the advent of greyhound racing, the greyhound was a dog bred and maintained exclusively for coursing purposes by private owners without any commercial element entering into the matter. The good greyhounds were, in the majority of cases, never offered for sale, their owners retaining them jealously with a view to breeding. Only when an important coursing enthusiast died or decided to give up the sport did the cream of the greyhounds of the country find their way to the public sales, but when they did high prices, even in bygone days, were realised. Even then, the highest authenticated price was one thousand and fifty guineas, paid for "Hung Well," a winner of the Waterloo Cup 1913. There were of course a number of breeders throughout the country who bred greyhounds for sale, and for the best, good prices were at all times forthcoming. The general custom, however, was that coursing men bred their own dogs and at great expense, expense altogether out of proportion to the value of the animals. They maintained them on walks from the time they were weaned until they were ready to come into kennels for training, usually in the April of the next year after birth. Seldom or never was it possible to purchase single individuals out of litters except at the sales, and even then an entire litter was usually offered.

Now, however, things have changed. Breeders of other breeds of dogs are taking up the greyhound cult, and on different lines from what has obtained hitherto. They are wise in their generation and, provided always they breed on the right lines, they are likely to find greyhound breeding a most profitable industry.

Up to the present no really good greyhounds have competed upon the tracks. The best greyhounds have not been necessary for racing purposes for, owing to the system of handicapping on times, any six dogs of fairly equal speed were good enough to make up a race, and, as it was necessary that all dogs had to be in the charge of the promoters of the various tracks, there was no encouragement given to prominent owners to send up their best. Now, however, that open stakes have been instituted, and it is possible for owners to take their dogs to the tracks just before racing and remove them the same night, it is quite within the bounds of possibility that gradually the very best greyhounds in the country will make their appearance on the race track. Gradually, too, a demand will spring up for the best and this is bound to greatly stimulate breeding activities. Racing will in no way affect the breeding of dogs for the coursing field, so that the present eight hundred odd litters will continue to be bred annually, but in addition to these an enormous number of additional litters will have to be bred for the tracks. How many tracks will function ultimately is a matter of the greatest speculation, but we can take it for granted that not less than thirty tracks will be in permanent operation in England and Scotland together. When racing eventually gets placed on a firm and sound basis, dogs will travel from track to track in exactly the same way that horses visit the various racecourses to compete in the races which their trainers chose for them and in which the latter think they have the best chance. To keep up an adequate supply of dogs for the profitable working of, say, thirty tracks, six thousand greyhounds at least will be necessary. This means that at least three times that number must be bred annually, for distemper, accidents, etc., will account for two-thirds of the number whelped. Taking the average litter as being six in number, some three thousand litters will have to be bred.

Furthermore, there is the rest of the world to supply. Practically the entire countries of Europe have fallen victim to the sport of greyhound racing, while America increases her number of tracks annually and does not appear to have the proclivity for breeding good greyhounds ; Asia and Africa are demanding and likely to continue to demand greyhounds from Great Britain and Ireland. It is a strange thing that Great Britain and Ireland would appear to be the most successful breeding grounds in the world. We have bred dogs of every kind for centuries, and other nations have purchased from us and yet do not seem to be able to produce their own from the imported stock. The same thing applies to blood stock and pedigree cattle. The greyhound will prove no exception to the rule. Our climate, no doubt, has something to do with it, and it may be that we know the art of rearing and management to a degree to which other nations cannot attain for many years to come.

The advance in the price of greyhounds during the last two years is almost unbelievable. The average class of dog on the track would, with difficulty, prior to the racing boom, have realised £5 each, and now we may take it that the average price is £40 and steadily on the increase. If we come to consider that the average price of the successful coursing dog was probably £100, his price, when he comes into common use on the track, will advance in like proportion and add another " O " to the figure.

There is no branch of live stock to-day which offers the same brilliant attraction as the greyhound. The Irish farmer has already grasped the situation, and it is no longer true that the pig is the gentleman who pays the rent. It is the greyhound now, and he is not only paying the rent, but the rates and taxes too. The English and Scottish farmer has not yet realised the profit there will be to him in breeding greyhounds. Many other people in different walks of life have embarked upon the industry, but the farmer of all men is the one who can most successfully carry on the work. He has what most other people have not, the indispensable space for the proper rearing of the greyhound. He has, too, in many cases, the adequate supply of milk so necessary to its proper growth. Of all dogs, the greyhound is the one which requires the greatest amount of freedom. His great activity makes it essential that he has space upon which to gallop and roam at will. His conformation and nature demands it from earliest infancy, and it is a fact that young greyhounds, if shut up, never do any good. Even in the first two months of life they can become malformed to an extent which it is for ever after impossible to counteract. The greyhound is one of the most peaceable of dogs, and is as happy as the day is long when wandering about on a farm. He is always delighted to accompany the farmer on his round of inspection, will follow the plough up and down from early morning until dewy eve, and, after that, is prepared to run the countryside with the children in their play. A life of this character is what suits the greyhound best and the only one which makes for thoroughly successful breeding. Professional breeders of other breeds will no doubt do well with greyhounds, but it is to the farmer to whom we have to look for the best-looking, best-reared greyhounds of the future. The opportunity to breed greyhounds has come to him at a time when his business is in as bad a state as it has ever been, and it is certain he can improve things a good deal by taking up the new industry.

For those anxious to make a start there is no time to be lost. The moment is as favourable as it ever will be. Prices are advancing, and those who begin now will reap greater profits than if they wait for another season. Good bitches are few and far between, and even now difficult to buy. Large breeding syndicates are being formed daily with comprehensive schemes for coping with the ever-increasing demand, but intensive breeding of greyhounds never has and never will be a great success. Breeding syndicates will learn from experience that decentralisation of their stock must be their motto. The promiscuous herding together of dogs invariably ends in failure, and in the case of the greyhound this is doubly true. In subsequent chapters it is the aim of the writer to advise breeders on the best lines on which to breed, and to assist them in avoiding the many pitfalls into which they are almost bound to descend unless thoroughly educated in the art of management of the greyhound.

## CHAPTER III

### WHAT IS A GOOD GREYHOUND?

" HANDSOME is as handsome does " is an adage as
true to-day as when it was first written.  Then what
" Handsome " is can probably be illustrated by
another old saying supposed to be descriptive of
a greyhound, and is as follows:

> " The head of a snake,
> The neck of a drake,
> A back like a beam,
> The sides of a bream,
> The feet of a cat,
> The tail of a rat."

It sounds like *hors d'œuvre*, but is in reality a very
apt description indeed.

To begin with the head :  Do not go to the Zoo to
inspect snakes in order that you may be quite sure that
your greyhound has the right formation of brain box, for
the simile is just a shade exaggerated, but in general
outline the shape of the head is as near that of the snake
as well can be.  The good greyhound has a nicely
flattened skull, with fairly prominent eyes and a long
muzzle with plenty of strength.  The teeth should be

strong and gleamingly white. The ears should drop nicely to the cheek and should never be pricked. Since greyhound racing came in we have perhaps seen more prick-eared greyhounds than we ever thought existed in the whole world, and although it is held by many that there have been various good track racers with pricked ears, it is a feature in the greyhound which should not be encouraged. It denotes a lack of quality and bad breeding somewhere, with too much suggestion of the bull-terrier blood at none too distant date in the past. If it were only the hideous disfigurement which prejudices one against pricked ears it would be nothing, but the look of the thing is only a symptom of some bad trait which is certain to crop up in the work of the animal.

Coming to the neck, we are again confronted with a simile which is perhaps a little far-fetched but one which gives us the right line. The neck should be long and muscular and beautifully symmetrical, with not the slightest suggestion of flabbiness, and it should be let into the sloping shoulders which, in the description above, are not mentioned. The general idea of the neck is that it shall be of sufficient length and possessing enough freedom in the shoulders to allow the greyhound to stoop in his stride and kill his quarry.

The likening of the back to a beam is perhaps the most apt simile of all. Everyone has seen a piece of timber just roughly squared up and with undressed corners. This is exactly the look which the back of a well trained dog should present. Because a dog may not have this type of back at a given time is not to say that it cannot be made. There are dogs, however, and plenty of them, which never will carry a back no matter how well handled and fed they may be. To make a perfect back is a fine art known only to the skilled trainer.

The " breamlike " sides is another good simile. It is more appreciated when the two can be compared. The chest should be very deep, going down almost like the keel of a ship but not to a sharp line at the bottom. The under part of the brisket should be fairly broad across. The formation of the sides (chest) should be of a character affording plenty of heart and lung room. That is to say, plenty of spring of rib together with depth of chest. There is a type of chest in which there is great spring of rib with very little depth, giving to the dog a barrel-like appearance. Although this formation of chest probably affords sufficient heart and lung room, it is certainly not to be preferred to the correct chest referred to. Then again there is the chest of abnormal depth with flat sides like two plates; this should be avoided always. A chest of this kind is frequently so deep that when the dog gallops his brisket will strike the ground.

As to the feet, you have only to pick up the first sleek-looking street cat and make a note of its feet to get the right idea of what the perfect greyhound foot should be. It is a remarkable thing how few bad-footed cats there are and how many faulty feet you can find in greyhounds. Lack of condition, however, can reduce a perfect foot in a greyhound to an almost unrecognisable travesty of what it should be. A greyhound which has had good feet that have subsequently gone out long and flat should not be given up in despair. With attention and a return to health and fitness it will be found that the feet will also return to their former perfect shape. To sum up: The feet should be of the shape of those of the cat; the bones should be stout and strong, with no lumpiness; the claws should be thick and strong and, on perfect feet, quite short, requiring no cutting; the pads should be very elastic and cushion-like, with a hard surface; the heel pad should fit tightly into the toe pads in such a manner that it should be almost impossible for the animal to pick up the smallest particle of grit; the correct stand should be on the toes, and a dog who is well on his toes is pretty sure to be in best and fittest condition.

In comparing the tail to that of the rat, the reference is to length and sparsity of hair. The quality of the dog shows out in the tail. Although there have been many good, game and distinguished greyhounds with thick and bushy tails, these latter are usually indicative of lack of quality. A good tail is frequently referred to as a whip-tail, and this again is another good simile; a really good tail felt with the finger and thumb, joint by joint, from top to tip, feels very like the lash of a hunting crop.

We have now exhausted the points as enumerated by the ancient inspired with a poetic turn of mind, but we have still to deal with a few very salient points in the make-up of our greyhound. His legs, for instance, are of the greatest moment. His front should be as straight as a gun barrel, with elbows close, but not too close to impede his action. They must be neither turned out nor turned in, and spring in the pastern joints is not desirable. With running, a certain amount of spring develops, but it should not be there at least in the dog's first season. Then again there are the hind-quarters, a most important part of the anatomy. The pelvis should be of great size with the tail set low, something that you can smack the hand across, with plenty of room to spare and without feeling anything but a level surface of flesh and muscle. It should slope gracefully from the pin bones to the root of the tail and present a square appearance.

The thighs should be big and thick like first prize hams and should be never flat or soft. The stifles should be well bent and the hocks low to the ground.

It has been said that a good horse cannot be a bad colour and this applies equally well to the greyhound, but as far as colour goes it is very occasionally that one finds a good blue. They lack stamina and are only too often without quality. It is in the blue dog that the ring tail or the corkscrew tail is most frequently met with and these defects, together with pricked ears already referred to, are sure indications that there is something wrong somewhere. They are marks of degeneracy as surely as the outstanding of marks of degeneracy in the human being. Apart from the unfortunate blue, colour does not count for very much in the greyhound, but the best of all is probably the red. A red is possessed of plenty of gameness, speed, and staying power. From out of the great number of greyhounds pupped every year, it is remarkable how very few really good ones come to the front. It is easy enough to breed good ones, but it is very difficult to keep them as Nature made them and even improve or rather help in her work. Management means everything and it is frequently more by luck than good judgment that a dog proves good in his early age. It is of course the survival of the fittest.

## CHAPTER IV

### BREEDING A GREYHOUND

UP till 1926 there were exceedingly few really bad greyhounds. When I say " bad greyhounds " I mean badly bred greyhounds. Great thought at all times was brought to bear upon the problem of how best to mate the good bitches of the country. Owners who were not expert in the art of determining the right blood to let into their bitches had excellent advisers, for the average trainer, in addition to being an expert trainer, was a past-master in the art of knowing the right way to breed a litter. Trainers, in a great majority of cases, are the descendants of trainers. Greyhound training is of all jobs the one which runs most in families. Greyhound knowledge can be said to be bred in them and they have an almost instinctive knowledge of everything pertaining to the breed.

Never before were there so many people interested in greyhounds as there are to-day, and, unfortunately, the great mass of these are starting the wrong way. They will give us in the course of a year or two the worst greyhounds the world has ever seen. They are breeding already on haphazard lines without a single thought of the scientific methods of breeding good stock. It

Photo by]                    [The Sport and General Press Agency.

" Golden Surprise " (" Jerrim "—" Bonnie Rig "), 1925 Bk.b., has run 30
courses, winning 27, including the Waterloo Cup, 1929, and the South of
England Cup. The property of Mr. A. Gordon Smith.

Photo by]                    [Thos. Fall.

"Demetrius" ("Denny"—"Latta"), 1924 Bk.d., has only run three times in
public, drawn after winning two courses at Altcar and ran a good second to
"Golden Seal" for the Waterloo Cup. The property of Lord Dewar.

"Paschendale" ("Guard's Brigade"—"Jassonia"), 1926 R.f.d., winner of nine races, he is from a stout coursing strain, inclined to stick too closely to the hare, which fault means he has superior speed. The property of Mr. W. H. Watts.

"Golden Splendour" ("Scoop"—"Waterweed"), 1925 R.f.d., litter brother to the Waterloo Cup winner, "Golden Seal." The type of the perfect greyhound. (See rhyme ' 'The Head of a Snake," page 26.) The property of Mr. P. Clancy.

makes one shudder with horror to hear the novice making statements about breeding which contravene every
law which has governed the breeding of greyhounds for
a century or more and have given to us year by
year better and faster greyhounds. Perhaps though,
during the last few years (prior to greyhound racing)
there has been a tendency to go too much for speed.
This is a controversial subject, so let us pass it by. Let
us pass by also further criticism or mention of the
mistakes being made by beginners, and instead try and
speak a word of advice to them, in order that they may
realise before it is too late the way in which they should
go.

To all those who have decided to breed greyhounds,
it is all important that they breed only from the
best. Buy bitches of the right blood and breed them
to the right dogs. By doing this, nobody can go very far
wrong. It is still possible to purchase bitches of first-
class breeding of three years old and upwards. Many
of these were picked up for a few pounds to make up
races on the tracks and, not proving very useful there,
have and are being sold daily. With reference to age,
the novice should not be afraid of embarking on a five- or
six-year-old bitch. The man or woman who has been
connected previously with pedigree dogs as distinct from
greyhounds is very sceptical about an oldish bitch which
has not had pups, so used have these pedigree dog
breeders become to breeding their bitches on the first

c

heat, the most iniquitous practice possible. Of course pedigree dogs of which no exertion is ever asked can afford to have their strength sapped by rearing pups before they have themselves passed out of puppyhood, but in the case of the greyhound it is a vastly different proposition. Good greyhound bitches do not start on their coursing career until they are sometimes as much as one year and nine months old, and, provided they run three seasons, they are over four years before they are available for breeding. If, therefore, any novice is offered a well-bred bitch which even at five years has not had a litter, no fear need deter him from making the purchase.

Having made the purchase, the next thing of importance to be considered is what dog will suit her best. The man of small or no experience should not be misled by others with no greater knowledge than himself. I some time ago sold a magnificently well bred bitch to a lady who was good enough, when the time came, to seek my advice as to the right dog. The bitch's pedigree was of the best and I had no difficulty in naming a dog—a dog, in fact, very closely concerned in the blood which produced the previous year's Waterloo Cup winner, "Golden Seal." My advice was taken, but the amusing thing about the matter was that a near neighbour of the lady, who had recently taken up greyhound racing, severely reprimanded her for not having sent the bitch to his dog, who was standing at four guineas as opposed to the fifteen she paid elsewhere. The man's dog was bred in anything but the purple, he had never won a course and, what is perhaps worse, he had never won a race, but was advertised as having run fourth to such good dogs as So-and-So and So-and-So. Advice such as that offered to the lady by the novice should be ignored. In breeding a bitch the owner should be sure that the dog he is going to use has at least got some kind of a win to his name. The sporting papers have always got a good list of stud dogs, and a perusal of these will be sufficient to put breeders in touch with the best dogs. It must be remembered, however, that it is not always the dog which is standing at the highest fee which will best suit your bitch. Pick out a dog which you think you can afford and then seek the advice of an expert as to whether, in his estimation, your choice is the right dog to serve your bitch. In the sporting papers the dogs advertised are seldom or never without a creditable record. There have been good stud dogs who have not won public courses, but in the main in such cases these dogs have been prevented by accidents from running : you can depend upon it that prior to their bad luck in breaking a leg or like misfortune they all ran good trials. If a bitch has not done much in the way of winning courses do not be too shy about her, for, provided she is made the right way and bred the right way, the less she has taken out of herself may make her the better brood, and the weaknesses in her can be counter-acted to a great extent by the dog to which she is put. Do not, however, run away with the idea that any kind of a thievish bitch can have all her degenerate traits corrected by the sire. Until the actual present, it almost appeared that all one had to do was to buy bitches and produce greyhounds to make a fortune, so low was the standard of the dog running on the track. Things have changed. Open races are here and will stay here, and for the purpose of open racing greyhounds of an ever increasingly high quality will be required. The breeder who produces rubbish will be left with it upon his hands, but the man who becomes known to produce the best will have for the rest of his life a large income and pleasant life. To sum up, buy the best and thereby breed the best. In the future nothing but the best is going to be worth possessing for racing on the track.

## CHAPTER V

### WALKS V. REARING AT HOME

AT the imminent risk of repeating myself, let me say again, up till 1926 greyhounds were required for coursing only, and were in the hands of men and women to whom money was no object. They had estates, or could have had estates if that would have improved their chances of winning the Waterloo Cup through being able to rear their precious greyhounds at home. Those people did not, however, go in for home rearing but put their greyhounds out to walk.

The majority of greyhounds were whelped and reared in Cumberland and the Border Counties. There were three main reasons for sending them to that part of the country. First, the climate from long experience was proved to be suitable. Second, the remoteness of the hills and fells from busy highways gave freedom to the valuable bitches which they could not have had elsewhere, and third and last, but not least, the people of the country understand the management of greyhounds, the secrets of the business having been handed down from father to son for centuries.

The rearing of greyhounds in these northern counties amounts to a great industry. There are men there whose trade it is to receive and manage the famous greyhounds of Great Britain. They are known as puppy rearers. They are known to trainers and owners, and every puppy rearer has his regular patrons. When the bitch is mated, she is sent direct to one of those men. He places her on one of his walks, in some lonely dale where the cottager or small farmer takes charge until she whelps and suckles her litter. When the whelps are eight weeks old the puppy rearer puts them out in ones or twos on to other walks, where they remain until the time comes for their going to the home kennels or to the public sales, which approximately will be in the March of the year after birth. It is a long and expensive business, but people breed always with a view to great distinctions and a definite object, and thought nothing of the cost. During the long period accounts are settled monthly with the puppy rearer. He receives from the owners or their agents the money due to the walkers and what the puppy rearer receives for himself in the end is £1 per sapling delivered fit and well at Carlisle station. It is a big and well organised job and one which is likely to continue while coursing lives. The system of walking in the North is the best and only one, that of entire freedom for the growing youngsters. They live in the cottages and go out and in at will. They accompany the master in all his jobs around the farm or garden. They romp when they want to and sleep when they want to, and there is no routine in the way of walks or exercise. The one thing which comes with the utmost regularity is the food, and that, on the recognised walks, never fails. Another important factor in favour of these counties for rearing is that hares are not too abundant, and wide and open spaces of flat land few and far between where the saplings, finding hares, might do themselves a life-long injury in coursing before their strength permits.

A fairly large number of greyhounds are, however, reared in the South, mostly in Kent. The system here is different to that of the North. It is generally carried on in paddocks specially set aside for the purpose. There is no organised scheme of things such as that just described as obtaining in the North, the work being carried on by certain small farmers and dairymen. Kent is very suitable, especially around Ashford and that district where there are many quiet places quite as remote from traffic as the quietest part of Cumberland. The Kentish lanes are narrow, with high and overhanging hedges and road surfaces which motoring fiends avoid. Roads and lanes such as these make the life of the greyhound fairly safe. Unless such places are found the growing greyhound stands a bad chance, for where there is much traffic, the walker is naturally afraid to risk the animals on the roads and, in consequence, they get insufficient exercise to promote the quick growth so desirable in a running dog. A favourite system of rearing in Kent is to set aside a paddock of an acre or two around which a six-foot fence is erected. In the centre of the enclosure there is a hut for the bitch in which to whelp and rear her litter. This system proves right up to the hilt that the greyhound is in nowise a delicate or pampered dog. The hut has no door. The idea is that from the moment the whelps can get about by themselves they shall have perfect freedom to wander forth and never be penned up. The hut is an open hut, but has a wind screen which cuts off all draught. That is to say, on the side of you when you enter the hut there is a partition which extends nearly from front to back and around the end of which the bitch has to go to get into her bench. It will be gathered that no matter where the wind is from it cannot blow on to the bench.

If a breeder has a few acres of land and some knowledge, of course, of how to rear, he can quite profitably embark on the Kentish system and rear his stock at home. From the time the whelps can run out they should be permitted to do so, and the state of the weather should never be considered. When it is wet, the whelps will not be too inclined to sally forth, but, if they do, it must be remembered always that they know their own business best. Let them at all times have plenty of deep bedding in their bench and see, too, that it is a big one—big enough to sleep the whole litter when they are full grown. The hut, it will be observed, is in the centre of the paddock. This is important. By the time the whelps are three months old and have found their legs, they will take to galloping round the hut. This is exercise of the best possible kind. At about three months they should be taken out, one or two at a time, just to have a look at the outside world, for dogs, like humans, will become shy if not shown the various strange things of the outside. They are bound to make a dead set at the feathered kind they see for the first time, but although they are not to be encouraged in killing poultry they should not be harshly chastised for so doing, for it has to be remembered that those greyhounds are required for coursing and are presently to be asked to go and kill their hares with fierce determination. If they can be broken of fowl killing without interfering with their natural instincts, so much the better, for it always deprives greyhounds of much of the freedom they would otherwise have if they are poultry killers. Even if money is forthcoming to settle the damage bill, walkers dislike the abuse they receive at the hands of the poultry keeper when their dogs run a-muck, and, in consequence, frequently leave the dogs at home rather than face further annoyance caused by their escapades.

The Home Rearing system is good enough, provided the breeder has not got too many dogs and has also sufficient open space for his stock. It is possible to arrange for the necessities of the bitch while in whelp, and for whelping her too, in a very small space, but space you must have for the whelps. Unless the whelps have their entire freedom from the time they are four weeks old, disaster is bound to enter the camp. There is no dog in the world which can go wrong so quickly as the greyhound. However much space you have in excess of one acre does not concern me, but one acre you must have. This one acre, enclosed for a litter in which it has absolute freedom, is worth more than a thousand-acre park in which it is given exercise twice daily. A litter which is shut up and taken out at intervals will never be a scrap of use to anybody.

The novice, therefore, must make up his mind which system he is to adopt. If he follows on the lines of this chapter he cannot go very far wrong, but if he thinks he can rear greyhounds as he would rear Pekingese, his bank balance will quickly inform him of the folly of his ways.

Until greyhound racing came we were entirely unacquainted with the trade in greyhound whelps. Now, however, greyhound " puppies," as the new people term them, six weeks old are being offered for sale in the same way as the terriers and cur dogs, and, on the assumption that there will be a ready sale at six weeks, many people are breeding on premises where one could not swing the proverbial cat. If they clear the whelps at six weeks all may be well, but wait until eight . . .

## CHAPTER VI

### THE WHELPING HUT

THE site for the hut should be in a sunny paddock with a slight southern slope. A wood to the north is always of advantage or, failing that, a good thick hedge which can be arranged for. The hut should be placed as nearly as possible in the centre of the paddock. It should have a good deep foundation of small cinders with a liberal admixture of broken glass as a fortification against the incursions of rats. The floor should be of good concrete.

The hut in dimension should be 12ft. by 12ft. The height should not be less than 6ft. to allow of comfortable standing-up room when visiting the inmates. The entrance to the hut should be on the east side, as fewest gales come from that quarter. The wind screen or partition should run from north to south for, say, 9ft. That is to say, on entering the hut the wind screen will be opposite to you, say, 3ft. away. To reach the sleeping quarters you must therefore turn to the left and walk along the passage to the end of the screen and then turn right to enter the screened-off compartment. The bench should be on the north side, and the south side should be well provided with glass windows

which should be made to open. It will be gathered
from the description of the construction of the hut that
it is impossible for the wind ever to blow on to the bench.
There should be no door. A lean-to roof will answer
the purpose perfectly and this may be covered with any
good felting, but corrugated iron should not be employed
on the ground that it is cold in winter and hot in summer.
Good stout timber should be used in the construction
of the hut, and as it is desirable to shut out all draughts,
a thorough coating of pitch outside is of great advantage.
The cutting draught which enters through chinks in
woodwork is very distressing to the dogs, causing them
to rest uneasily from continuous efforts to get away from
the annoyance. It is on all occasions a good idea to
line the inside of the hut for about 3ft. up from the
floor and around the extent of the bench.

The bench should extend across the entire width
of the hut, which, if we allow 3ft. passage way, will be
9ft. From back to front it should be not less than 3ft.
6in. This may appear large, but it must be kept in
view that your litter is more likely than not to be eight
in number, and eight greyhounds take up a considerable
space if they are to be allowed to stretch themselves
out. This bench or platform should be made in sections
to afford greater facility in removing it for cleaning
purposes. It is unnecessary to have it more than about
12 inches from the floor. If, however, the height desired
is sufficient to permit of a dog going in below, a bar or

two should be run across to prevent this happening. A face board of 10 to 12 inches should run across the front of the bench to keep back the bedding.

The bench just arranged for is designed for the comfort of the growing litter more than for whelping purposes. A much smaller space should be allotted to the bitch as a nest. About 3ft. 6in. by, say, 4ft. will be ample. A large packing case of that size and about 2ft. deep makes an ideal nest. If a box of this type is to be used, it can stand on the bench. It is a good idea while the bitch is in whelp to take one side of the box out with the exception of the bottom plank, which should remain to keep back the bedding, but after the litter has been safely delivered the side should be built up again. This makes it more comfortable and ensures against the whelps scrambling or rolling out later, when they will be able to climb up and fall over. It is better to remove the boards as before so that in the event of a whelp getting over in the night he will have no difficulty in getting back.

The floor of the hut should have a good deep covering of sawdust or chaff, or the sweepings-up from a hay loft. It makes cleaning possible and absorbs moisture, and, in the event of a whelp reaching the floor, it is, especially when chaff is used, a protection for him from the chill of the concrete.

With reference to the suggested glass on the south side, this is intended for all the sun possible being thrown upon the bench, but it must be made to open, for in summer time the whole hut will become too hot, and, provided the weather is warm, greyhounds cannot have too much air.

As to the fencing of the paddock, 6ft. wire will be ample, but it should be made to lean inwards at the top. If this be done, dogs will be the less inclined to try and jump out. Pig wire is the best. If stapled strongly to a wood frame it will last for years. The frame makes a neater and more enduring job, for the wire does not sag as it is certain to do when merely taken from post to post.

When you have provided yourself with a hut and fenced paddock as described you have the main essentials for breeding and rearing the strong, healthy and the upstanding kind of greyhound which is required.

## CHAPTER VII

### MANAGEMENT OF THE BROOD BITCH

THE best type of brood bitch will be dealt with in another chapter and at present we will confine the subject to the practical management of the bitch. The choice of a sire is also a separate subject and will be gone into later. The premier factor for the moment is the right time of the year to breed. The advent of greyhound racing has, up to the present, put at naught all the established theory on the subject, but presently, when things simmer down, breeders of racing greyhounds will fall into line with the practices observed by the coursing fraternity, and to get litters as early in the year as possible will become the aim and object of every owner. Before racing came, litters whelped after July at the latest were of little or no use, because they were not ready to run in fair competition the year following with the others whelped at all times of the year from January on. Coursing, with its large produce stakes run usually in September, October and November, made owners concentrate on bitches which came on heat as soon as possible after the end of October, so that January whelps could be got. January whelps, if they do have to put up with cold and wintry weather, score over all the whelps of subsequent months when it comes to September twelve months after birth, in the matter of age at least. March whelps are probably the best, owing to the fact that by the time they leave the dam they can have the advantage of getting the sun on their backs and from the benefits derived in this way make up rapidly for the two months or so they have lost to the whelps produced in January. There will be little to chose between these March whelps and the January whelps in the September twelve months after their birth, but every month subsequent to March is attended by an additional handicap to the whelps so born. We do not as yet know what the new body of control for greyhound racing will decree as to the seasons for the new sport, but it is anticipated that winter racing will be stopped and that the seasons will be from the time coursing ends until the time when coursing re-commences. That is to say, racing will take place from March until September or October. If this rule should be made and produce stakes be introduced into racing, which is bound to be the case, then it will be the aim and object of owners to get July litters. This will mean that with coursing on the one hand and racing on the other, there will be all the year breeding going on, each sport providing for its own requirements. This, if it should happen, will give us very quickly two distinct types of greyhound, for a dual capacity animal will not be aimed at. However, as at the moment we do not know what The National

Greyhound Racing Club is likely to decree, we must lay down lines for breeding just as though racing did not exist. After all, the racer has to come from the coursing blood, and we may take it for granted that it will be a very long time before the coursing dog is taken from the racing strains. If we adhere to established principles of breeding, we shall breed dual capacity greyhounds. Breed as though for coursing and you will not be wrong. If you breed a coursing star, he or she will always be worth money. If he or she falls short of the standard in the coursing field then there is the track, and many greyhounds, which up to the present have proved failures in the coursing field, have attained to great success on the track. It is a different game and calls for different qualities.

The time to put the bitch to the sire of your choice is any time after the ninth day subsequent to the first symptoms of heat. The duration of heat is twenty-one days and provided that you are sure as to the first day when heat came on it is perfectly safe to leave the mating until the sixteenth day thereafter : if the matter be left until then, there is no doubt that there will be a predominance of dog whelps.

After mating, the bitch should be kept confined until all symptoms of heat have vanished. If not in the enclosure arranged for in the previous chapter, she should be led out for exercise in order that she may be free from molestation on the part of dogs. Even if

D

she is introduced to the paddock at this time and she has not been accustomed to it before she should be taken out for exercise.  She must of a necessity be alone or with another bitch or bitches (a choice of two evils), for in the former she will mope and distress herself adversely and in the latter may fight or be fought by the others of her sex, as they will molest as badly as dogs.  When heat has passed off the bitch should be given quite a considerable amount of the paddock.  She can then, of course, have a dog with her for company, in which case one will amuse the other and the exercise afforded by the paddock will be sufficient for her requirements, but a walk in human company is always appreciated and of great benefit to the bitch.  She should, however, sleep in the hut every night during pregnancy.

Presumably, before being mated, the future matron was on one feed per day, in the evening.  After mating she should have two feeds daily, a light morning meal of bread and milk and her usual feed at night with as much, if not a little more, flesh than she has already been receiving.  The breeder must be careful, however, in not increasing the meat ration unduly.  The addition of a liberal milk allowance to the ration will be sufficient to meet the increased demands upon the system of the bitch.  If an adequate flesh ration has been allowed before mating it need not be increased, but even with the milk addition the flesh should not be decreased.

For seven weeks the bitch can lead her normal

life, but after the end of the seventh week it is wise to remove other dogs from her in case of fighting or being violently run into while at play. The paddock at this time will be of the greatest use, for the bitch can wander at will and can, in addition, be taken out on the lead for a quiet walk and some consoling intercourse with the owner.

The nest should be kept provided with plenty of good clean wheat straw at this time. A greyhound bitch, as is the case with all breeds of dogs, will scratch away all the straw and place her whelps upon the floor whatever it may be, so it is important that the floor should be of wood : this will be the case if the details of the last chapter are adhered to. The bitch removes the straw in order that she may be able to clean up the evacuations of the whelps, which it would be well-nigh impossible for her to do were the straw left under them. This eternal cleaning up she will do for at least three weeks.

The process of parturition is accomplished with more ease in the greyhound than in any other breed of dog. The whelps are small in comparison with the size of the greyhound. Cases of whelping trouble are few and far between, and the necessity of offering assistance to the dam is in the majority of cases altogether unnecessary. What cases there are, are mostly due to a strain from galloping or jumping, and even this is not always attended with serious risk, for I myself had a bitch which ran a rabbit and killed it and then went back and delivered six strong healthy whelps within the hour. Another I had jumped at a pigeon on a low bough, caught it and ate it and successfully whelped eight whelps overnight. Such occurrences as running rabbits, etc., are to be avoided if possible, but provided the bitch is fit and well little harm may ensue.

The greyhound is a prolific animal and may give birth to anything up to fourteen whelps so it is always wise to have a foster mother in view. A bitch in good condition should be able to suckle eight whelps. If the litter should exceed that number a foster should be employed. A breed of similar weight to the greyhound should be used. Small terriers, etc., are not to be advocated. Greyhound whelps grow rapidly and become as big if not bigger than a small terrier foster. The quality of the milk does not vary in the different breeds of dogs, but it becomes difficult for the greyhound whelp to get a sufficiently fast flow of milk from a diminutive foster mother. Setters, collies and the like are most useful, and the cross-bred animals of similar size are invariably first-class fosters. That the temperament and nature of the foster is imbibed by the greyhound whelps in the milk is an exploded idea which is not worthy of a moment's consideration.

The greyhound is a splendid mother and perhaps more than any other shows greatest reluctance to leave her litter for the briefest space of time. From the first day, however, she should be encouraged to come out and empty herself, a duty which she will neglect rather than leave the whelps. At ten days or so she should be taken for at least a half-hour's exercise twice daily. This must be on the lead, for otherwise she will hurry back to the kennel before going any appreciable distance.

Devoted mothers though greyhound bitches are, having much hardship to suffer from the teeth and claws of their offspring, they tire of them, I think, more quickly than any other breed with which I have had any experience. To relieve matters as much as possible, it is an excellant plan to cut the claws of the whelps when they are a fortnight old. By that time these punishing little claws will have taken the shape of hooks and the hook part should be cut off with scissors, which greatly saves the udder of the bitch. The milk teeth are phenomenally sharp, and the jaws being of such strength in the greyhound the suckling litter inflicts great pain and suffering on their thin-skinned mother, causing her frequently to desert her family as early as at three weeks. It is well therefore, almost as soon as the whelps can see, to accustom them to having their muzzles dipped into cow's milk. They like the taste and quickly come to lap from a saucer. At three weeks they will be lapping strongly and can have the milk thickened with flour. They may also have good broth from sheep's head thickened in the same way, so that if the bitch should desert her family they are in a position to do without her. She should, however, if everything goes well, remain with the whelps until they are six weeks old, but at that age the bitch should be removed entirely.

While the bitch is with the whelps, after three weeks, they should, in addition to what she gives them, be fed three times daily. Owing to what the bitch has to endure from the whelps she cannot be depended upon to let down to them what milk she has, so that the three feeds a day puts things on the safe side. If the whelps are in any way purged, the milk or broth should be thickened with arrowroot or well-boiled rice.

At three weeks a 'strict watch should be kept on the bedding. While the whelps are not moving from the bare space cleared for them by the dam, she herself will do all the cleaning up, but immediately they begin to move about and soil the straw she is helpless, and it is then that the kennelman must lend a hand, and he will, if necessary, have to give fresh straw twice or three times daily and never less than once daily.

The feeding of the bitch during the suckling period is most important. For the first three days after whelping she should be kept on a milk diet. Plenty of milk with not too much bread is best. Two quarts per day will be required. It should be given warm with bread crumbled into it, or, perhaps better still, bread which has been scalded in boiling water. A little sugar is much appreciated and at the same time beneficial.

After the third day, if there are no signs of fever, the bitch should be put back gradually to her original food and to the amount of flesh to which she has been used. She should be fed at least twice daily. Milk should be given in addition to her usual food throughout the period of nursing her litter. A well-fed brood bitch should leave her litter in better condition than that in which she was before whelping. The time at which a bitch usually looks thinnest is just before whelping, and bitches which leave their litters thin do not do so because of the strain which has been put upon them, but because they have not been properly nourished or been given sufficient food.

If medicine has to be resorted to while the bitch is suckling the whelps, there is nothing better or safer than castor oil for those ailments such as purging, which frequently assail the bitch.

## CHAPTER VIII

### REARING THE WHELPS

WEANING, the whelps having been eating now for at least three weeks, should present no very great difficulties, or be attended with any great risk. Because, however, you have managed to possess yourself of a six weeks' old litter from the best blood, and have already begun to conjure up pictures of a Waterloo Cup or a greyhound Derby, you must not forget that your troubles have not as yet begun. There are a thousand and one unforeseen militating factors which may creep in, causing your brightest dreams to vanish in a flash, and yet, upon the other hand, it is positively astonishing how a whole litter will attain maturity without a single day's illness of any kind. Having decided that the enclosure and hut system of rearing is to be adopted, you stand every chance of being amongst the lucky owners just referred to, for absolute freedom goes far to help the litter through without disease or accident. Freedom and good rational diet are the two greatest factors in the successful rearing of a litter. Feeding after the removal of the bitch is the thing of greatest importance. The whelps should be fed at least four times daily.

" Up in the morning " should be the motto of everyone who has set out to rear greyhounds or, for that, who has anything to do with greyhounds. The first feed should be at six in the morning, the next at eleven o'clock, the third at four o'clock and the last feed at nine in the evening.

The food will be much the same as that which the whelps have already been partaking of while with the dam, except that the flesh off the sheep's head should now be added to the food. This should be broken up and not minced. The fragments should be about the size of a horse bean. The broth will now be thickened with oatmeal, good brown bread, one or other of the recognised puppy meals (of which there are many on the market) and have the fragments of meat mixed in. The food should be fed warm but never hot. One sheep's head per day will be sufficient for a litter of six until they are ten weeks old. Whenever purging makes its appearance, always thicken the broth, etc., with well-boiled rice. This must, however, be well boiled for, if otherwise, it is a most harmful feed. The same remark applies to oatmeal which, in moderation, is a most excellent article of diet if properly cooked, but the reverse is so frequently the case that it is almost with some reluctance that I now advocate its use. Oatmeal badly cooked, instead of being the great aid to growth which it should be, is a deterrent and is responsible for any number of puppy disorders. While on the subject of oatmeal, I cannot pass on without remarking that many people have an exaggerated idea of its worth. It is a well-known fact that wonderful greyhounds come from Scotland which have been reared on porridge, but it is well to mention here that the Scotsman's idea of porridge is a vastly different proposition to that of the Englishman. When the Scot feeds porridge to the dogs, it is with floods of milk, and this is the secret of the whole affair. Porridge with milk is a perfect food. Porridge with a little meat added is not a perfect food. If a good supply of milk is available there is no better food than the porridge and milk of Scotland. To make the porridge as it is done in Scotland allow one pound of oatmeal to six pints of water. Porridge in England is cooked in a double saucepan for hours and in the end is a very tasteless and sloppy dish. In Scotland it is cooked fairly rapidly but the making amounts almost to a ritual.

The water is brought to the boil in an ordinary iron pot, salt is put in and then the cook, with the " spirtle " in her right hand and the meal box on her left, begins operations in earnest. Seizing a handful of the meal she trickles this through her fingers into the boiling water and simultaneously she begins to stir, and as handful after handful goes in, the stirring never ceases. She does not of course weigh a pound of meal and measure six pints of water, she knows to a nicety when the porridge is ready. This comes from experience, but, roughly

speaking, when she feels that the concoction is sufficiently thick she puts in no more meal but goes on
stiring for a while longer until the porridge begins
to spirt up in blobs. If one of these happen to get
you on the hand you know the porridge is cooked.
The farm hands when making their porridge allow
more than the pound or, which comes to the same thing,
do not use so much water, so that in consequence their
porridge is much thicker, and this as dog food is better.
I am afraid that an apology is due from me for going so
exhaustively into the science of making porridge, but as
I have never seen the matter thoroughly described in
any book on the dog it is perhaps an opportune moment,
and, provided that people will follow instructions, it
will relieve my mind as to the harmful results which
may come from feeding oatmeal in the wrong way.

I have become very enthusiastic that the growing
whelps should eat a certain quantity daily of good sound
biscuits. There are various excellent puppy biscuits
on the market and one cannot go far wrong in making
a purchase. If there is purging amongst the
whelps stop the biscuits at once.

The first great enemy which the whelp will now
encounter is the worm pest. There are few, if any,
whelps which do not contain worms. There is little
doubt but that the majority of whelps are born with
worms, but as a general rule they do not make themselves pronouncedly objectionable in the whelp until

about eight weeks old, but many deaths at a much earlier age are due to them. If, however, worming can be postponed until the whelps are eight weeks old, so much the better. At that age I strongly recommend that all whelps be wormed, even if they be doing well and do not appear to require it. No matter how well the whelp may look, it is one in a hundred from which worms do not come after a good vermifuge. Worms would appear to be the inheritance of the dog. Although he may be thoroughly cleansed to-day, in a few months a fresh invasion is made upon him and so it goes on as long as he lives. It is important therefore that the whelps be cleansed at the age mentioned, for then they are relieved of the greatest stumbling block to their satisfactory growth. Whelps full of worms cannot go ahead, and notwithstanding the best of food they go off in condition and as a rule waste away and die : if they do not die they grow up into misshapen weeds of no use to anybody. There are so many excellent preparations now manufactured that it is almost a waste of time to prescribe for worms in the whelp. Whichever preparation is used, it is most important that the instructions of the manufacturer be rigidly adhered to. Many disasters occur in administering vermifuge which are due entirely to carelessness in a non-observance of the instructions supplied with every bottle or box.

The motions of the whelps should be kept under the closest observation. The colour and the condition of these are the surest guides to the health of the animals The motions should be of a ginger-bread colour, neither white nor black. If the latter be the case there is nothing to worry about, but if white, it is certain that there is something wrong with the diet. More flesh is necessary, but if black it means that too much flesh is figuring in the ration and it must be reduced.

It frequently happens that whelps at from eight to twelve weeks will go suddenly off their feed and stubbornly refuse to eat. They are runny at the eyes and are supposed to have distemper. The medicine bottle comes into use. The whelps are drenched and put on to milk food, from which as a rule they turn with more disgust than from the food to which they have been used. Hundreds of whelps die annually in this way, when all that is required is a change of food from that of which they have had a surfeit. The following solution to the problem does not always work, but it will nine times out of ten. Briefly, substitute fish for meat and watch results. It is unnecessary to purchase the best parts of fish, for what is appreciated most by the whelps is codhead or other large fish heads. Your fishmonger will always be able to let you have a large head, but as there is not much demand for heads see that what you get is sweet and fresh. Boil the head in a piece of muslin, strip off all the fish and separate carefully from the bones and let the whelps have it warm. They will nearly always fairly bolt it down and if they do you will know there is no distemper. If they take to the fish you can, after the second feed, introduce some well-boiled rice with it, but it is better at first to let them have the fish without anything so as not to discourage the fresh desire to eat. Whenever whelps fall ill, the one great idea is that they have got distemper. Whelps, infested with worms, will exhibit all the symptoms of distemper, and it is indeed a fact that more whelps die annually from worms than from distemper, while there are other stomach disorders from which can come symptoms hard to differentiate between those of distemper. A constant change of diet is at all times necessary, and although the dog is a carnivorous animal it is well for a couple of days at a time to knock him off meat and substitute something else. Fish one day, and plenty of bread and milk, or porridge and milk another. In summer time, when butter-milk is available, use that occasionally. There is nothing better for the blood.

At twelve weeks three feeds a day will be sufficient, but the quantity will have to be increased. The late meal should not be discontinued. It need not perhaps be given so late as previously, but the night feed is always desirable as the whelps settle down afterwards and do not move much until the early morning. This practice will be kept up until the whelps are six months old, when the feed will be reduced to a light meal in the morning, and the main feed of the day in the evening, and at this time each whelp should be receiving a pound of meat per day together with his meal or biscuit.

At around sixteen weeks the whelps will begin to shed their milk teeth. This is often a very trying period, and especially if they have been wrongly fed. If, however, the whelps have been properly managed, beyond a slight falling off in appetite, due no doubt to the discomfort in eating, there need not be any great trouble. It is always helpful to look over the mouths and assist out any loose teeth which the whelp appears to have difficulty in shedding, but do not force it out. They will come by themselves in time. It is most unwise to interfere too much with the mouth. If a whelp is badly pained in having teeth removed he will be shy ever afterwards about having his mouth opened, and this is sometimes fatal in illness when it is necessary to give a drench. I knew one greyhound who had been so hardly treated in having teeth removed, that it was impossible during the whole of his life to give him a pill, and on one occasion, when it was a matter of life and death, it was a physical impossibility to open his mouth : other means had to be resorted to, less satisfactory, and only saving his life at the last gasp.

The education of the whelp is important and should begin at an early age. One of the chief drawbacks to the enclosure system of rearing is that from the time the whelps can get about there are many familiar sights to which the farmyard whelp becomes accustomed from his earliest moments entirely unknown to the enclosure born animals. The litter whelped in a stable and sallying forth for the first time into the stable yard stands every good chance of seeing poultry and, more or less growing up with the hens, never has any inclination to kill them. In fact, the whelps are as a rule put in their place by some fiery old broody hen, which does not cow them but which merely teaches them a lesson in good behaviour. Horses, cattle and sheep they have access to, and by instinct they learn that all such stock is the property and care of the master, just as they are themselves, so that without chastisement to guide them in the way in which they should go they grow up to respect the property of the man to whom they owe allegiance themselves. The enclosure whelps are not in so fortunate a position. They have never seen poultry, pigs, horses, cattle or sheep, except occasionally through the meshes of their wire enclosure, and they have either been seized with fear of the larger beasts or with the desire to kill the smaller. As the whelps should be taken out to see the world when they are three months or so old, great care must be taken on the first few occasions : everything that moves will be investigated, and if it is found to contain blood a great deal of tact and discrimination on the part of the keeper will be brought into play. There are people who can communicate to dogs their disapproval of bad conduct without having actually to resort to thrashing, but such men are born

" Kreisler" ("Three Speed"—"Waltz Away VI"), 1925 Bk.d., of unusually powerful build. Holder of track record for 500 yards at Shelbourne Park. Winner of the Empire stakes and other races. The property of Mr. J. W. Boyle.

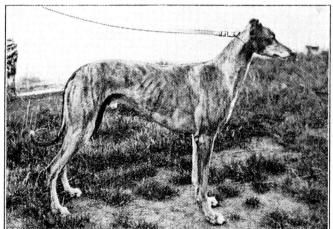

" Kilrush" ("Lax Law"—"Kitty Hastings"), 1926 W.bd.d., was second to " Kreisler" (beaten half a length) in the Empire stakes at Wembley, June 22nd, 1928. The property of Mr. J. W. Boyle.

*Photo by* ] [*Photo Press.*

"Blackheath" ("Guard's Brigade"—"Kaiser's Girl"), 1926 Bk.b., a winner on the flat and over hurdles at Harringay—possessing all the attributes for success in a racing Greyhound. The property of Mr. D. D. C. Giddins.

*Photo by* ] ]*Daily Sketch.*

"Past History" ("Face the Foe II"—"Cheerful Nell"), 1925 Bk.d., winner of seven races and two matches over 400 yards—record breaker for that distance at Clapton. Shortly being retired to the Stud. The property of Mr. J. Nathan.

and not made, and the majority of people, not being thus born, then a certain amount of thrashing will have to be done. If the whip has to be used let it be a whip of very light make. A hunting crop is much too heavy. Use a whip which will sting without causing anything in the nature of a bruise. A riding whip of the lightest possible design will answer the purpose admirably. A sharp cut or two with this, accompanied by the reproving voice, will accomplish as much as a severe hiding, and this latter a greyhound must never have. He will be expected at no very distant date to pursue the hare with fierce determination and kill her, too, if necessary, so it is no use to expect that, if he has been severely chastised for an attack on poultry, which the whelp cannot be expected to respect, having never seen such things before.

On these first excursions into the world there is always a danger that the proud master may take his party too far afield. Although the whelps at about this time will be weighing twenty to twenty-three pounds and looking fairly big dogs, it must be remembered that they are very young babies and easily tired. They will have plenty of spirit and will follow for miles, but if they are permitted to do so they will suffer for it later. A short ramble along a quiet lane, with a visit to an adjacent field, will be all that is necessary for the whelps, which should be returned to the enclosure before they exhibit

E

any signs of fatigue. Any whelp which seems to take no notice of chastisement when poultry-killing or sheep-running should be put in a box muzzle. This type of muzzle occasions little or no inconvenience to the whelp, and often is the means of preserving in courage a great greyhound who, without it, would have had all fire and boldness thrashed out of him because of his proclivity for waging war on one or another of the farmer's stock. In any case, accustoming to the muzzle is more important nowadays than it ever was before, for sooner or later every greyhound destined for the track will have to wear a muzzle of one or other pattern, and there is little doubt but the box will become the standard.

Collars and leads, if they can be avoided, should not be used before the whelps are six months old. When, however, they have attained that age they should have lessons in their use. Let them wear collars to begin with for short periods at a time, and when they have had them on once or twice and have been led out of the enclosure with the fingers through the collar, then one day slip on the lead. When the whelp, bounding forward, finds himself a prisoner he will probably rear high into the air and then dash himself to the ground and go through a variety of bad-tempered antics, but the best plan is to allow him to try everything he can think of to either free himself from the encumbrance or, what is more probable, to play upon your feelings so that you will in pity release him. When he realises that all is of no avail he will come along, still pretending, perhaps, to be very determined not to put up with the nuisance but really quite reconciled to the new conditions. After two or three days' schooling in this way the average greyhound will walk in a dignified manner which would not disgrace him in Bond Street. There is always certain to be a puller in the litter and he is a great trial. It takes a long time to subdue this tendency, but subdued it must be, for it is a most serious problem. Pullers cough and grunt through the pressure which they bring to bear upon themselves from the collar, and they are as likely as not to pull and cough when put into slips, and it can be imagined that a dog who enters upon a course in a fit of coughing has little or no chance of ever overtaking the hare or even getting level with his rival. Such dogs should be taken out by themselves and sharply jerked back by the lead whenever an attempt is made to pull. This can only be done satisfactorily when the dog is alone. If he be in a string it is probable that through leads being twisted some innocent dog gets the jerk, the delinquent going scotfree and unaware that he was to have received a reminder of his bad behaviour.

The collar should be of the wide variety, shaped out for the throat, and not the usual two inches all round, as these collars are very hot and confine the neck unduly.

When thoroughly trained to collar and lead the whelps should be taken out on the roads once daily, and walked at a slow pace for not more than half an hour. The prime object of taking them out at all is to accustom them to traffic and unfamiliar sights, but, provided that they are well-grown and in good condition, the hard roads will have a beneficial effect in hardening the feet. If, however, the whelps are in any way weakly, the effect on the feet will be the reverse and they may be spoiled permanently. When a dog is well and strong his feet will be hard, dry and rough to the touch, in fact, there is no more certain test of condition. Conversely, when the feet are putty-like in consistency, smooth and dampish to the touch, you can be certain that all is not well. The condition of the animal is reflected in the feet in no less a degree than in the eye.

At from eight to ten months, it is better to remove the litter from the enclosure and put it into kennels. All important as is the complete freedom of the paddock up to this age, comparative confinement for the future is necessary. For the first few months, the young-sters invent games for themselves and play all day in galloping up and down the complete length of the paddock, or chasing round and round the hut, and vary-ing this with rolling one another over in wrestling matches upon the ground, but later they want more grown-up amusement and cease to take an interest in childish things. They do not, therefore, in the paddock, exercise themselves sufficiently, but when put in kennels they come out fresh, take tremendously fast gallops on being released, and thereby thoroughly exercise every muscle.

The road exercise should now be increased to three hours per day in two spells of equal length, one in the morning and one in the afternoon, while grooming should begin, both with the hands and with the glove. Grooming while they are yet in the enclosure is neither desirable or beneficial. Coats are required to carry all the natural oil possible as a weather resister when they are much in the open. If, therefore, grooming is indulged in the whelps suffer much more from penetration of the wet.

After the evening meal, free exercise in yard or paddock is essential. This should always be given even on wet nights and the dogs dried down on return. There are many greyhounds which will not empty themselves in small kennels and suffer greatly therefrom.

## CHAPTER IX

### MANAGEMENT OF THE SAPLINGS

OUR whelps having now attained the age of twelve months will be known as " saplings " until the beginning of the season, when they will be known as puppies and remain as puppies until the end of the season.

If they are January whelps, they attain their first birthday at a somewhat awkward time of the year for being taken into training kennels, because in January all the leading trainers are in the midst of their season, with the Waterloo Cup only a few weeks off.

The saplings, therefore, may have to take these few weeks extra before entering on the first stage of serious work. However, the Waterloo being over and only one or two big stakes yet to be run before closing the season, trainers begin to find kennel room and time for the reception of the youngsters. Each trainer is sure to have some dogs still left in training, and as private trials yet have to be run the saplings are afforded an opportunity of seeing the older dogs running hares and thereby getting their first taste of what they will participate in themselves in the autumn of the year.

Entering the saplings to their game is of the greatest importance, and if at the time of coming into training quarters they should not have seen a hare previously (which they should not have done) no time should be lost in giving them a chance of so doing. If the saplings have been well reared and are of the right strain, a hare at twelve months in the case of dogs, and ten months in the case of bitches, can do no harm.

As to whether the sapling runs his first hare in company with another of his own age or with an experienced but slow dog of greater age is a matter whereon there is a difference of opinion, but I myself would always let two saplings run together, for if they are bred the right way they will take to their game like a duck to water. An older dog, even if slow, has experience with the hare in his favour and is more likely to kill the hare than is the sapling, which is disheartening to the latter. A kill for the sapling is a great event too, for the dog can then be patted and encouraged with the voice, which he never has been after running sheep, cats or poultry, and will feel that at last he has found something to run which is legitimate for him to kill if he can. The dog is of course greatly pleased and never likely to forget this first happy experience in destruction. Being satisfied that the sapling is game and possessed of good pace, which will improve, he ought to be put aside in reserve for the ensuing season.

Too many hares, if the dog is destined for the

coursing field, spoil his chances, for a greyhound learns, only too soon, what it is to run cunning.

Too many hares, if the dog is destined for the track, is impossible. Up to the present the mechanical hare, on all the leading tracks, runs on the outside. The tracks are, on an average, some twenty feet wide, so that the circuit of the outside is very considerably greater than the circuit of the inside. Now, a dog which has not learned to run cunning will pursue the electric hare on the outside, whereas a dog who has run long enough to use his brains more, will manœuvre for the inside and, even if not possessed of the pace of an honest dog keeping on the outside, will beat him by virtue merely of having travelled a shorter distance.

The saplings have now the pleasure of a summer ahead before taking up their real work in life, so that the intervening months will be spent quietly and pleasantly in unofficial walks and plenty of play in the paddocks and fields. It is better to keep the saplings apart as far as possible from the older dogs. The older dogs domineer over the saplings in kennels, and, as a rule, interfere with their play. If all together on the road when they have only to follow along the two lots have little chance of getting to loggerheads, but it invariably happens that when saplings and older dogs are released together in a field, trouble ensues. The saplings want to gallop, but the older dogs, who are too lazy to indulge in childish play, nevertheless hate to see the saplings going a big pace and will run up and bite them out of pure jealousy. There is no dog living more jealous than the greyhound, and this jealousy is indeed one of his chief qualities, for without it we would not have the sport of coursing. It is the jealousy of one dog towards another which makes the brace work each one for himself in the course to try and kill the hare.

The saplings which have been tried and found wanting have, happily, nowadays the race track waiting for them instead of the knock and the hole behind the kennels. Up to the present, the more important tracks have declined to accept saplings, so that owners buying these from the kennels from which they have been discarded, have a task of a different kind of sapling management from that applicable to the dogs which are going into training for coursing.

The future racer can be allowed much more freedom. It is immaterial whether he kills rabbits all day long, and it is a matter of congratulation rather than otherwise if he accounts for hares whenever opportunity presents itself. One thing is certain, if a dog which has never had a kill is put on the track he is not likely to win a race. He may race with great speed up to a point, but he is deficient in a finish. I think that greyhounds are not so stupid as to look upon the mechanical hare as a thing of life, but I do believe they would like to catch her.

There seems little doubt, however, that the style

of running by the dogs on the track tells us plainly that the dogs themselves regard the race as play, and do not bring into it the grim determination exhibited by dogs while running a hare. That they are not concentrating on the mechanical hare as they would do on the real thing accounts very largely for the frequent fighting which takes place in races. . . .

Now that so many racing enthusiasts are starting establishments with private plants for working mechanical hares both types of sapling can, with advantage, be tried round the track occasionally during the summer months. This will have no detrimental effect on the dogs which are ultimately going to be coursed, and will be of great advantage to the future racer. The speed of the hare will at all times be regulated to the condition of the dogs. It is a first-rate mode of exercise, and when all is said and done an improvement on the hand gallop, of which more will be said later. It must be kept in view, however, that this kind of work should not be carried to excess. A lot of it will prove more detrimental to the dogs intended for the track than to those who are to be coursed, for it is well known how quickly racing dogs become stale. To get them stale to the game while yet saplings would be disastrous, but in the case of the others getting stale at the mechanical hare matters little, for what work they do in that direction is only regarded as a simple mode of exercise to save labour. The early morning should be chosen for exercise on the track. It is a temptation sometimes for the edification of friends to have a few races in the afternoon, but on hot days it amounts to cruelty of the worst kind.

The saplings, provided they have been managed previously according to the methods as laid down by me in preceding chapters, should not come in fat, but there are greyhounds so robust that no amount of exercise will reduce them in weight. It is not desirable too early in the summer to get them to their proper weight, so that this should be done very gradually. Dieting, if they are too gross, can be attended with no harm to the constitution.

Farinaceous food makes fat. Flesh and milk make for a decrease in fat. If flesh and bread be the diet and the saplings are fat, cut down the bread and increase the meat. The colour of the fæces will advise you as to whether your proportions are right. If too much flesh is being given the fæces will be black. Porridge and milk or bread and milk can be made in such proportions as to reduce fat. A large ration of milk and a small proportion of the farinaceous part will keep a dog perfectly healthy and nourished and at the same time reduce fat. Dogs (and human beings) can live on milk alone but will become as thin as the proverbial rake. A dog cannot, however, live on bread alone.

A sharp outlook must be kept for worms, which should be removed whenever they make their appearance. If all these things be done, and the saplings can be kept happy and high spirited throughout the summer, the work of training will already be half done. A fortnight to three weeks will suffice for strong work, but if the preparation of fat dogs has to be undertaken as the first step to work, it will be six to eight weeks before the dog can run.

## CHAPTER  X

### KENNEL  CONSTRUCTION

BEFORE passing on to the all important subject of training, it will be well at this juncture to investigate the two main plans upon which kennels are built, for after all kennels are as important to successful training as the most scientific methods of bringing the greyhounds to their best for coursing or racing.

I have my own unshakable opinions as to the best type of kennels, but I am not going to be in any way partisan and will describe each impartially.

I am going to take first the older plan of kennel, which is a long range of six kennels of about the size of loose boxes for horses, the fronts facing south and opening into an enclosure of about one acre. Each kennel will be in dimension, say, ten foot by ten foot. The cookhouse is in the centre, with three kennels on each side. The cookhouse is entered from the north and has, of course, a door into the yard on the south. The enclosure is be fenced round with a ten foot fence, so when the cookhouse door is locked everything is under lock and key. The cookhouse, if of the same dimension as each kennel, will be big enough for all useful purposes, but it can be as large as the owner cares to plan. Under this system of kennelling, six or eight dogs are kennelled together in each house, the theory being that if this number of dogs and bitches mixed are kept together they agree better and fight less than when two only are kennelled up in the same place. This principle being accepted we have kennel-room for at least thirty-six.

The kennels should be built of stone or brick and the floors of glazed tile, and each kennel should be lined with the same tiles for at least three feet up. The present day concrete block with a damp course is perfect, and might be substituted with advantage for stone or brick. The height to the eaves should be at least seven feet. As light is most beneficial a window on the north side should be arranged for and the doors should be provided with a grill and a sliding shutter, so that on calm days a free supply of air can be afforded to the dogs. There should also be glass on either side of the door, protected by an iron or wire grating and designed to open, but not necessarily so. The window on the north side should, however, be so constructed as to admit of a through draught with the aperture in the door.

The bench which extends across the entire back of the kennel should be constructed on the lines of a trough, high enough at the back and ends to prevent the dogs from lying against the cold wall of the kennel, and nine inches at least in front. It need not be more than one foot from the ground, but in this case should be made so that it can be removed for easy cleaning underneath. A bench of this size is a heavy affair and should rest on battens which extend for at least five or six feet beyond the width of the bench towards the door of the kennel, so that the bench can be slid along when cleaning has to be done. The bench should be at least three feet from back to front. Many experts like to have the bench raised at least three feet from the floor, but this is unnecessary ; being so high it often leads to fighting at night through a dog jumping up and on top of a sleeping companion. If the bench is as high as I suggest, a dog is not so liable to jump in awkwardly and annoy his fellows. A paved pathway along the front of the kennels is always a convenience, especially in wet weather.

If each kennel be ten feet wide and the cookhouse the same, the frontage will be seventy feet, or, roughly, twenty-three yards. If an acre is arranged for on the farm, the turning-out yard will be about 200 yards long. It should be of grass, and every effort should be made to keep it so. Some people prefer a square yard, and this is easily arranged. You have merely to carry the high fence some twenty yards in a straight line from each end of the frontage of the kennel and you get nearly enough the one side of a square which will represent one acre (seventy yards each way). Mathematically, this is not absolutely correct, but near enough for our present purpose.

The other system of kennel construction is to utilise a large barn or similar building and build into it the necessary kennels. This system has its due number of disciples and there are certainly many distinct advantages in its favour.

Many old barns which have been converted into kennels were of such enormous size that kennels for fifty dogs could be arranged for, and space enough left in the centre for a covered exercise yard. Usually, under the barn system, dogs were kennelled in pairs and not in sixes and eights as referred to previously. Unfortunately, large barns nowadays are few and far between, and to acquire one would probably mean that an estate of a couple of thousand acres would have to be purchased. It is possible, however, to build something on the same lines. The best plan to be followed is as described below.

First, select a site for the kennels, sixty feet long and thirty feet wide, with wooded shelter on the north, if at all possible, and with no barrier to the sun in the south. Upon this site it is proposed to erect kennels for the same number of dogs as are accommodated in the plan first mentioned. The area of the site in the second case is just twice as great as in the first idea, which makes a material difference in expenditure, but the extra outlay is compensated for by the very distinct advantages gained under the system.

The material for the walls should be stone, brick

or best concrete blocks. Floor to be of best glazed tile or unabsorbent concrete. The roof to be of good tiles put on in the usual way. Under the tiles there should be a ceiling not less than eight feet from the floor. Five doorways to be arranged for as follows. At the eastern extremity of the north wall, and western extremity, and in the centre of ditto. The two other doors will be in the south wall directly opposite to the doors at either extremity of the north wall.

We have now got the shell of the kennels which we are going to divide up into eighteen kennels, two entrance and exit passages, one cookhouse and one office.

Fifty-five feet of the entire length of sixty-five feet will be occupied by the kennels, cookhouse, central corridor and office. The ten feet out of the length provides for a five-foot passage at each end of the building, with opposite entrances in each, one in the north and the other in the south wall. It is now required to construct eighteen kennels, each five feet by ten feet, cookhouse ten by ten feet, office ditto as follows :

Having allowed five feet for passage way, build down against the north wall five kennels five feet by ten feet, cookhouse ten feet by ten feet, four kennels five feet by ten feet.

Against the south wall, build as against the north wall, substituting the word office for cookhouse.

We have thus got eighteen kennels, ten at the east end, and eight at the west, separated from the larger

F

section by the cookhouse and office. In both sections of the kennels a ten-foot gangway will run between the two rows of kennels, and at each end of this gangway or corridor there are to be doors closing the whole from the end passage-ways, cookhouse, etc.

It will be gathered that when all doors are closed, the central portion of the building will consist of three compartments, each ten feet by ten feet. That is, cookhouse, office and a vestibule between the two, and separating one section of kennels from the other. The kennels are so designed that in the case of illness one lot can be entirely isolated from the other. The door from the vestibule into either section can be locked and sealed up and disinfected sheets hung up as an additional safeguard, and the affected kennels handed over to people who will have no occasion to enter the other section or even the cookhouse.

The lighting will be by a window over each kennel, but this will have to be fairly high. Each window should be fitted with an iron grill and made to open outwards. For further ventilation, shaft ventilators in the centre of the corridor will be found to be best.

The partitions dividing the kennels should be carried to the ceiling and may be of concrete, but in that case should be tiled for three feet from the floor.

The bench to be of the same pattern as already described.

Two grass paddocks will be arranged for, one on

the south side and another on the north. By this means it will be possible to keep the dogs of each section apart, even at exercise.

In my opinion the kennel just described is the most ideal in every way. It is entirely free from draught, but light and airy, and, for convenience in working, cannot be rivalled. In feeding in bad weather there can be no comparison between the under-one-roof system and the door-to-door arrangement without having to go into the cold and wet yourself or even admit the cold air to the dogs.

As far as possible, it will be well to kennel a dog and bitch together, but if greyhounds are comfortably housed and well fed they are not quarrelsome, so that there is not much to fear from having two of either sex kennelled together.

Artificial heating is not necessary. Greyhounds will appreciate any quantity of heat and always appear to enjoy an overpoweringly high temperature, but if they live in a hot-house they suffer for it when in the field. Kennels such as just described can never be too cold, and in the case of the first system, where many dogs are kept in the one kennel, they lie so closely together on cold nights that they keep one another warm.

The question of clothing is one upon which opinion differs widely, but I myself am one of the disciples of the advocate of clothing. It is not only that the dogs enjoy it, but I am convinced that it makes for better condition.

Drains in kennels are always to be avoided. Things go wrong with these and bad and nocuous gasses come back. I would therefore advise the floors being slightly sloped towards the paddock or the corridor, as the case may be, so that when swilling out, the water will run clear of the kennel. In the case of the corridor all swill coming from the kennels can be swept to the end passage and then out. The floors of kennels and corridor alike should be kept well laid with good pine sawdust. This absorbs moisture and prevents excreta from adhering to the floor.

# CHAPTER XI

## TRAINING

WE are now about to tackle a subject the principles of which are known to few, and to a smaller number still the skill and experience how to carry them out. I am about to lay before the vast army of recruits to the greyhound cult the main features of training that animal. I cannot, however, hope to make every reader a famous trainer, but trust that the following pages will contain information which will be found of great use to the majority.

The preparation of the fat dog will be the first thing to occupy our attention. It will be noted that this subject has been dealt with as regards the saplings, which we assumed were in the home kennels being gradually prepared, but the time comes when you have fresh dogs to tackle, which are required for stakes early in the season and probably only a fortnight or three weeks off.

The weight of a dog, from his size, make and shape, will be named by the experienced trainer to within half a pound at any stage of condition, but it will be necessary for the novice to weigh his dog, after which he must proceed to reduce him to his proper running weight. The hand and the eye are, of course, the surest guides as to the time when the desired result has been attained. It will easily be imagined that an overweight dog can be brought down to weight and at the same time be less fit to run than he would have been when pig-fat.

The reduction of fat can be brought about in three different ways. Firstly by medicine, secondly by starvation and thirdly by work.

Physicing, whenever possible, should be avoided. Inside fat can be removed very quickly by its means, but the digestive organs are upset, and while they are recovering their tone the dog is not improving, but, on the contrary, will be getting soft.

Starvation is not to be strongly recommended, but it is certainly preferable to physicing. What is fat? Why is it there? It is a provision of Nature as against future exigency. If, therefore, the greyhound is deprived of a large portion of his food, what happens is that he immediately begins to draw on his own fat to supply nourishment for himself. This he can do without upsetting digestion, or losing muscle. This applies not only to the canine race, but to ourselves as well, the only difference being that the dog has been proved to have the proclivity for going without food for a longer period than any other animal.

Work, of course, is the proper method for getting rid of fat. Work makes a demand upon the tissues of the body, calling for their constant supply of fresh material, so that in this natural way the fat becomes

utilised in the manner for which it was intended.
Nothing can be better than that.

Now when we say work, we lead on to one of the
chief subjects in the larger one, called " Training."

A dog which has been lying about idle for months
must be put into work very gradually, and he usually
has to be taken in hand and prepared for what is expected of him. A fast or long gallop is as likely as not
to ruin an unprepared dog for the rest of his life, and
many have died within a week. Whether the dog is
above or below weight after a spell of idleness, the first
thing to do is to empty his stomach by means of an
emetic. A piece of common soda about the size of a
hazel nut, gently slipped down his throat, will produce
the desired effect in less than one minute. The dog
will in this way get rid of bile of which he may have an
excess. Vomiting in the dog is a natural process which
he will produce for himself whenever he can in season
by eating certain grasses. The next step is to clear the
bowels. This should be done on the following day with
a mild purge, which should be given in the morning,
and two hours later he should be given a bowl of brown
bread soaked in weak broth. If then taken out for
exercise, the broth will cause the physic to act, after
which the patient can be returned to his kennel where
he may remain for the rest of the day with the exception
of a few moments in the paddock before retiring for the
night. If any trace of worms is observed in the motions,

steps must be taken immediately for dealing with these. On the following day the dog should go on the road, walking five miles or so if under weight and up to ten miles if over weight. On being returned to the kennels his legs and feet should be washed in warm water, great attention being given to the feet for signs of soreness. The dog which is under weight will be given a ration of such proportion of bread and flesh as will tend to raise the weight. The over-weight dog will be given food of the same constituent parts, but will have an increase of flesh and a smaller proportion of bread. On the following day, exercise should be on turf consisting of some free play and walking on the lead alternately for a matter of three or four hours, but during this time the trainer will see that his charges keep steadily on the move, never sitting or lying down. On returning, the legs and feet will first receive attention as before, and friction be applied to the whole body, from neck to hind-quarters. Feeding will be as usual. On the following day as little walking on the lead as possible will be given, just that amount which has to be in order to get the dog to some adjacent training ground, where an hour's play will be allowed, and after that he should be tried on a gallop. This gallop should be up-hill.

The method of hand-galloping greyhounds is as follows :

The trainer will hand the dogs over to his lad, who

will be wearing a stout leather belt around his waist. To this belt he buckles the leading straps of the dogs to ensure that none manage to escape. Having thus secured the dogs, the trainer proceeds up the hill for a distance of, say, three to four furlongs, the lad and dogs following at a much slower pace so as to keep the attention of the dogs on the trainer. When a suitable distance separates trainer and dogs, the trainer whistles and shouts and encourages the dogs to come to him. When they have become anxious to do so, the boy slips the fastest dog. If this starts well he allows it to get twenty yards start or so before he slips the second, and so on until he has released the " string." The trainer picks up each dog as he arrives and puts him on the strap which is ready for him. Some excellent racing is to be seen in this way, for the dogs will go to a sympathetic trainer with more gusto, I think, than that with which they go to the electric hare. To see a dozen or more dogs engaged in a gallop of this kind, up a gentle grassy slope, is as pretty a sight as one might wish to witness.

The gallop being over, the dogs are returned to kennels with all expedient haste to have their legs and feet well washed, and each in turn to be thoroughly rubbed down from stem to stern with the hands and with the gloves. By the following day some slight change will have taken place in the condition of the dogs. The fat contingent should have lost a couple of pounds apiece and the light members should have put on a pound at least, but it is more easily taken off than it is to put on. Digestion, heart, lungs and feet being all in a satisfactory condition at this stage, work in earnest can begin, according to the trainer's views on the question. Different men have different systems and the varying length of the daily exercise is staggering in its maximum and minimum. In the middle of the last century the work at the outset of training would amount from fifteen to thirty miles a day. When behind a horse the greyhounds trotted one half of the journey, then galloped as fast as the horse could move for a couple of miles and then walked home. Strenuous exercise, surely, but things have changed. Coursing has changed and is to-day a much shorter and sharper affair as regards pace than it was in the middle of the last century, when long trials were much more thought of than they are to-day. Greyhounds to-day are bred for pace more than for endurance, and are trained accordingly.

On three days of the week the greyhound should be walked upon the road anything up to twelve miles, but the distance will be dictated by the condition of the dog. Some strains can stand but very little road work, where others would appear to be able to stand any amount. So marked is this difference in different strains that an expert trainer knows before putting a dog to the test whether or not he will stand road work. On the other three days the dogs will play and hand gallop as described above.

When the greyhound is dead fit he should present the " back like the beam." It should be so square and level that an egg put upon it will not roll off. The coat should be as sleek as satin, the skin very loose, the dog himself the while looking as though he were ready to jump out of it. A dog which looks jaded is for a certainty doing badly in his work. There is something amiss or he is getting more work than is good for him. The dog not ready to bound off his bench in the morning requires close observation and should be taken in hand. There are, of course, the sleepy dogs who by nature are inclined to be lazy, but one gets to know them and to realise that they only exert themselves when it appears to be worth their while. A dog, however, not of this kind, who is constantly tired after extra strain, if he does not respond to treatment should be thrown out of work until his condition changes.

The bitches are the greatest trial of the trainer's life. They invariably come into use at the worst possible times and always when they are most wanted to fill a nomination in a stake in which they can win. After being in use, a bitch is seldom or never worth her salt for three or four months afterwards. Some, of course, the sexual trouble affects but little, and provided they are kept walking during their three weeks of heat may go back into training again and do well. Such bitches, however, are the exception. The majority become slack, put on flesh, and at the time at which they would normally have their whelps, carry milk : this they will continue to do for a further period of three or four weeks, which would be the suckling period had she been put to the dog and had whelps. As so many bitches are known to be so constituted, it is at a great risk that any bitch is kept in training after being in use. If hard worked, and particularly hard run during such times, bitches are frequently little further use either for coursing or breeding. It is wiser, therefore, even if it is at the loss of a coveted trophy, to put the bitch out of work. Greyhound bitches nowadays are seldom bred from until they have finished their running career. Fifty years ago, to breed a bitch and run her afterwards was common, but training to-day has been brought up to such a pitch of perfection that there is little chance for a bitch whose stamina has been weakened and her shape altered through having a litter of whelps.

Private trials before bringing greyhounds out is a part of training to which must be given the very greatest attention. Most trainers have their own training ground adjacent to the kennels, over which they run their trials with a view to ascertaining which dog is fast and which is slow. By means of running through a stake made out of the dogs of his own kennel, the trainer speedily gets to know his best. The experienced trainer, having become a judge of pace, is quick to note any dog with phenomenal speed : when he sees this he will probably keep it a secret and bring the dog out a big surprise to all. If, however, he has nothing outstanding in his string and is a wise man, he will arrange trials with other dogs not of his own kennel in order to discover how he stands with dogs of form, which have run well in good company.

The novice would be well advised to run as many private trials as it is possible for him to arrange. He has not had the necessary experience to detect outstanding merit in his dogs and is prone at all times to regard his geese as swans, and later, when he is a poorer but a wiser man, will realise how bad was his judgment.

Before fixing dates for private trials the novice should have already well tried his dogs to hares, for if they go to their trial green, it will be wasting the time of the trial dog without any useful decision being arrived at. There are those so impressed with the imagined excellence of their own property over that of everybody else, that they will remain unconvinced of the inferiority of their dogs even in the face of a trial, in which a dog has won with a stone in hand, so to speak. Such people scream their dissatisfaction and clamour for another trial. which sometimes is granted, sometimes not. It is impossible for me at this juncture to pass on without recounting very briefly what happened once at what has become an historic private trial.

A celebrated coursing man, who has a wonderful trial enclosure on his estate, had in his kennels a dog which looked a potential Waterloo Cup winner. Now by the consent of the owner in question, his private trainer was allowed to take a few dogs for other people. As the trainer was a man of great standing in his vocation, he got the best greyhounds to train. This, of course, was a matter of moment to his master, as all private trials could be run at home without anyone being a bit the wiser of results. Now at the time under discussion, amongst the dogs which the trainer had from outside sources was one, the only danger in England to the big hope of the kennel above mentioned. On a memorable occasion, the magnate, having issued invitations to some of his boon companions to attend trials in the enclosure, the two crack dogs were tried together. This plum of the morning was kept to the last and was run off just before lunch. The home dog was beaten fairly and squarely and in the outside dog was the Waterloo Cup as certain as day follows night and that death comes to all.

The trainer having returned his dogs to kennels hastened out to send a telegram to his patron, advising him of the result of the trial and to get his money on at once for the big event. On his return he found a message awaiting him that his master wished to see him at once. When he presented himself he was greeted with the following, " We are not quite satisfied with the result of the trial. Would it in your opinion do any injury to either of the dogs if we were to run it over again? " " Not one bit. Would you like the dogs now, sir ? " was the trainer's brief reply. " Yes, please, we are ready."

The dogs were speedily brought to slips, a hare driven up and off they went, the outside dog with the same advantage in the lead, and it was odds on him winning as he did before. At the turn, however, down he went, uttering the most painful yelps, but almost before one realised that he was down he was up again like a game dog but had one leg swinging. He had stepped in a hole. Enough said! The other dog won the Waterloo Cup.

Having referred to private trial enclosures, although these are beyond the reach of most, a slight description may not be amiss.

An ideal trial ground is fifty acres or so of an estate with two or three spinneys at fairly wide intervals. The acreage referred to is enclosed with a high wire netting fence in order to keep the hares at home. Each spinney is also wired in and game traps are fitted into the fencing. These traps are brass panels, say, twelve inches long and three to four wide. They are made to cover apertures in the fencing, or, rather, to fit apertures. A slit just a shade wider than the trap is cut in the netting and the trap suspended therein on a hinge at the top. The trap swings each way and can, when desired, be pulled right up, leaving free access to the hares to go out and into the spinney at will. The hares will, as a rule, live, in the spinneys so that on the morning of trials the ground is walked over and any outlyng hares are disturbed and driven to cover. When the ground has been cleared as far as possible the traps are let down and fastened, with the exception of two or three which are opened when the trials are ready to be run. The keepers then go through the spinney beating up the hares, which run for the traps. Finding this first one fastened, they look for the next opening, and when it is seen that a hare is in the open the keepers prevent other hares from leaving the spinney until wanted. Great trials of speed are carried out in this way, for the hare, never having very far to go, has practised himself in putting up a tremendous race for the next spinney. They are to all intents and purposes trained hares. They know where they are going and go there with a will. The ring fence is fitted with traps also, so that in summer hares can go to and fro at will. These enclosure hares are in no sense of the term boxed hares. It is largely from the use of the private enclosure that the fallacious statement is current in many directions even to-day that hares are taken to the coursing meetings in boxes. This remark does apply to rabbit meetings, but that of course is a subject outside the pale of common humanity.

Good level fields, however, where there is no wire, will answer perfectly for the private trial, and indeed most trials are so run. Trials on Downs are unsatisfactory and attended with too much risk. They are

"Spittle Rover" ("Gobby Fawn"—"Coursey"), 1926 Bk. w.d., winner of nine races at Cardiff G.R.A., including one Sweepstake of £100. Ran into the Final of the Welsh Derby. The property of Mr. E. H. Watts.

"Divra" ("Guard's Brigade"—"Golden Haidee"), 1926 F.b., winner as a puppy of a 16 all-aged Stake at Dorchester, and an 8-dog Stake at Rochford, only times run. Now at Clapton. The property of Mr. E. H. Watts.

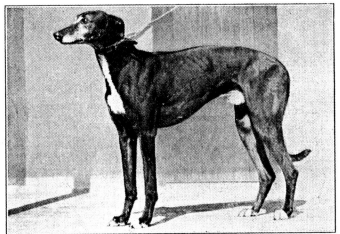

*Photo by]*       *[Bert Cooper.*

"Good Poacher" ("Jamie"—"Barbican"), 1926 Bk.w.d., has twice beaten "Chain Mail" and considered to be the fastest dog now at Harringay. The property of Messrs. Gilbert and Pollack.

*Photo by]*       *[The Sport and General Press Agency.*

"Golden Seal" ("Scoop"—"Waterweed"), 1925 Bd.d., winner of Waterloo Cup, 1927. In all, winner of 19 out of 20 courses. One of the most brilliant greyhounds of recent years. (As a sire suitable for both coursing and racing bitches.) The property of Mr. A. Gordon Smith.

unsatisfactory in this way, that the hares have never very far to go before going up-hill, and in so doing they score heavily over the dogs. Young dogs particularly stand too much chance of being over-run in such country. Another drawback is the great number of hares. A dog already hard run may pick up a fresh hare and yet a third before he has gone many yards.

The management at meetings is no small factor as between success and failure. Having been taken from home for private trials will have given the dog some little experience of travelling, and the trainer should have observed what effect this has had on the various animals under his charge. Most kennels have a motor van which is used for taking the dogs to meetings by road, a proceeding most of them enjoy. Provided that they do enjoy the experience, there is no necessity for getting them to the running ground until the actual day, but in the case of nervous dogs, or those which suffer from sickness while motoring, it is better to get them settled down a few days before at the place of a meeting. In so doing, however, the change of altitude is a point which has to be taken into account. Dogs which are trained at a considerable elevation will run well on ground of a lesser altitude during the first two days after being removed there from their upland home, but after two days, when they have exhausted the reserves of oxygen stored up by them from living at a high altitude, they become slack and lethargic. If, therefore, a nervous dog from

G

the heights is removed to something nearer sea level, say, three of four days before the meeting, although he may have settled down to his new quarters and become quite at home, he will in time suffer from slackness owing to the change of elevation. The only thing to be done in this case is to remove the dog quite ten days before he is required in order that he may become acclimatised by getting his respiratory organs used to the new conditions. This question of altitude is a scientific subject which has been gone into with great thoroughness in America with reference to the running of horses, and proved beyond all doubt to be a fact. A dog, if trained at an altitude of 700 feet, when sent to run on ground at 200 above sea level, will hold a distinct advantage for forty-eight hours over dogs trained at the elevation or a less elevation than the coursing ground. The dogs trained at an elevation the same as that at which they have to run are unaffected, but dogs coming from a lower to a higher elevation are affected adversely. Although mechanical vehicles have been brought to a pitch of absolute perfection, it is as well to get greyhounds used to trains, both as to travelling by train and seeing them. Things have a habit of going wrong, and motor vans are no exception to the rule : if the motor van does go wrong at the last moment, when it is frequently impossible to get another, the dogs have to be hurried to the railway station to make the journey by train. If they have had no previous experience this may upset them inordinately and completely ruin what otherwise might have been their Waterloo Cup. I would rather travel dogs by rail than by ordinary car, in emergency. In a car dogs do not settle down well. They become cramped and, especially if there are two or three, they do not rest. One dog used to car travelling, if allowed to use the seat, will coil up and make himself perfectly comfortable, but as a rule it is hardly worth while for big establishments to take a single dog to a meeting. The motor van should be a commodious vehicle with ample room for the dogs to lie well stretched out in the width, and high enough for the trainer to stand upright. This is very important, for at the meetings he can use his van in which to do everything necessary for the dogs, without any discomfort to himself.

Two people at least must attend the meeting with the dogs. There is plenty of work to be done, but even if the trainer is going to do everything himself, there should be a boy at least to be in charge of the other dogs when the trainer takes a runner up to the slips. If there is any access to the dogs, they may be got at maliciously, or, what is equally bad, they may be fed by thoughtless, inexperienced visitors to the meeting, who, out of the goodness of their hearts, think that a portion of sandwich given to a greyhound is doing him a kindness, but, on the contrary, many a dog with the best chances has been stopped in that way.

On the morning of the meeting dogs should be out

at six o'clock, and if at all possible given some free exercise in an open field in order that they may empty themselves thoroughly. It is often with the greatest of trouble that a greyhound can be persuaded to do this on the lead in strange surroundings. If, however, he can be let loose for a few minutes, the desired result can usually be effected. To make sure that nothing is picked up by the dogs when so set at liberty, the precaution of muzzling is always a wise one.

On returning to the temporary quarters after exercise, all dogs should be well rubbed down and then given a very light meal of milk and egg. The egg must be new laid, for if not it had better be withheld. That a dog will run better if no food be given on the morning of running is a fallacy. It is very seldom if ever that the first brace goes to slips before half-past nine, so that a light feed of egg and milk given say at 6.30 has long since been assimilated and has imparted its reviving properties to the dog.

When the moment arrives, the trainer will take the dog to the slips, leaving the collar on until the slipper has affixed the slip. The trainer then retires and holds himself in readiness to proceed in the right direction to be as near at hand as possible to pick up his dog at the end of the course. Having picked him up he will then return to his van or barn with his charge and thoroughly rub him down and apply embrocation as a safeguard against stiffness for his next course. Clothing will then be put on and the dog made comfortable. Many trainers nowadays give their dogs a raw egg after the course, and it is a rational idea.

Good trainers usually carry with them to the meeting all the food necessary for their dogs during the two or three days as the case may be. The hamper usually contains new laid eggs, a leg of mutton beautifully roasted, a cowheel jelly as clear as crystal, and plenty of toasted brown bread. There will be, in addition, the embrocation, fever mixture and the first aid outfit.

The articles of diet will meet the entire requirements of the various dogs.

Trainers who do not possess a motor van should make arrangements ahead for hiring one for the meeting, whether it be motor or horse-drawn. At many of the big meetings there is neither house nor shed within a mile, so that some shelter for the dogs must be provided. If, however, as at some meetings, there are farm buildings at the disposal of the trainers, a cab or other closed vehicle will suffice for conveying the dogs thither, but a private van is undoubtedly essential if the dogs are to be kept peaceful.

The end of the first and second day of the big meetings is determined as a rule by the light, which, when it fails appreciably, naturally makes the decision of courses difficult. The dogs, on returning to their kennels, should have another good dressing. They should then be fed and settled down for the night with a very liberal supply of good straw. In the majority of cases benching will not be available, but to make up for the lack of this, trusses of straw should be placed on the floor of the stall or box and the loose bedding put on top of these. This makes a capital bed. The dogs are raised from the ground, and with the thickness of a truss of straw between them and the ground there is no possibility of either cold or damp.

On returning home from the meeting it is always advisable to administer a good purge either late on the night of return or early next morning and feed for the next few days on a somewhat light and sloppy diet. No serious work should be undertaken by those dogs which have run and won, or for that matter by any which have run, except, however, in the case of dogs which on a weak hare got beaten before they were given any opportunity of straining themselves.

Training for racing as it at present stands is a somewhat different proposition from that for coursing, with which we have just dealt. As time goes on and open stakes become general on the tracks, the training of the dogs will be taken more seriously. To ensure programmes and full races, the early promoters had to stipulate, in accepting dogs, that they had to be kennelled in the Company's kennels and be under the Company's control to run in the races they chose, and in general they were to have the entire management of the dogs while on their premises. The tracks are all situated in the heart of great cities where it is difficult to exercise greyhounds, so that the system of training became only that for which there was facility. On the tracks where extensive grounds or gardens exist the dogs are walked about for an hour or so in the morning and afternoon : varied with this they get a gallop on the track itself when participating in trials. The exercise is sufficient to enable the dogs to acquit themselves creditably in a race, but were they in the midst of the season suddenly switched off to Altcar to take part in a coursing meeting, I think it most unlikely that they would cover themselves with much honour or glory. However, the extent of a race is prescribed, and provided that the dogs are kept tolerably fit, through all having the same kind and amount of exercise, they run fairly level. Certain race trainers who have had no coursing experience assert that the correct condition for a racer is soft condition, but this I strongly deprecate. Dogs which have come straight to the tracks from good coursing trainers have invariably done well from the first time of asking. That is, always provided that the dog takes to the game. " Grouse " is a typical instance of this. He was in strict training for coursing and in tip-top condition. He was a good dog to the hare, but after the turn was unable to keep from cutting about. As this is an incurable fault in a coursing dog, Captain Gladstone sold him to the track, where he was an unqualified success from the outset. Had " Grouse " not had the fault referred to he would have gone far in the coursing field. He was in the best of condition when he arrived at the White City, and, as luck would have it, he proved himself a natural racer. He left the gate in his first trial like a dog who had been months at the game and never looked back. His superb condition was a mighty factor in his favour and rather puts at naught the theory that racing dogs should run big and soft.

The famous "Entry Badge" is another instance of a dog who always ran in best condition. Although it is not generally known, I can now state with authority that "Entry Badge" was not kept in training at the White City. When not engaged in races there, "Entry Badge" was in the hands of Mr. Baxter's own private trainer in his own kennels in Kent and was brought up to the track when required. Had Mr. Baxter felt that the exercise and training possible under the conditions at the White City to be sufficient, he would not have had the dog at home under strict training. "Entry Badge's" achievements are well known and require no comment. He, too, was a born racer and always knew the advantage of manœuvring for the inside place. Sooner or later, most dogs will run on the tracks straight from their trainer's kennels. By keeping a certain number of spare dogs in the track kennels, to fill up gaps when entries are thin, the present régime of training on the ground will come to an end.

The future training of the race dog for open stakes

should present no great difficulties to the man who has knowledge of the other kind of training. The great aim in preparing a dog for the track is to make him a sprinter. The amount of road work required for getting a dog ready for coursing is not necessary in training for the track. Eight or ten miles a day at the very outside will be enough, and the rest of the work will consist of sharp gallops of distances no greater than the circuit of the track. The feeding will be slightly difficult to meet the requirements, but good hard condition will always tell. Practice from the trap need not be overdone. When the dog has once learned to get away, he will get plenty of practice on the various tracks to which he will be taken during the season. It seems highly probable that in the near future greyhounds will have programmes mapped out for them just as is necessary in horse racing. With reference to horses, there is a sound maxim that the best training they get in the way of gallops is what they get on the racecourse, and the same remark will apply to greyhounds. Too many gallops can be left at home. A 500 or 525 yards race as compared with a course entails very little exertion on the dog, hence the idea that they can run big and soft. No great muscular effort is required, the main thing being wind, and this they can quite reasonably have even when fat, simply by reducing the flesh ration and substituting farinaceous food in its stead.

The feeding during training for coursing must be of

such a character that the muscles, the nerves and the circulating systems get their due proportion of what they require. Without muscle, strongly developed, the greyhound will lack the power to exert himself in outstripping his rival, and without nervous energy he will be unable to make the attempt. If he be deficient in blood of the right quality, his powers of respiration will be deficient. To make muscle, fibrine and gelatine are necessary. The brain and the bones must have phosphoric acid and phosphates, and for the making of blood, more fibrine and albuminoids must figure in the diet.

All these materials are to be found in flesh and bread. Horse flesh (free from drugs) is good, beef is better, and mutton is the best—these three meats to be lean. The best bread for training purposes should be made from three parts of whole wheatmeal and one part of oatmeal. The lean flesh of the animals mentioned above, combined with the bread just prescribed, will contain everything required, but it is well occasionally to add some vegetable matter. Vegetables of the cabbage variety are not much use, and experience goes to show that leeks are most beneficial and onions are also of great value. A week or so before running, a few boiled potatoes have been found to impart freshness to the stomach. The bread should be fed stale, not in less than seven days from being baked. Biscuits which contain first grade flour and oatmeal in the same proportion as that advocated for the bread make a welcome change. A constant change of diet is demanded by the greyhound, and trainers are first-class cooks and most ingenious in ringing the changes in the use of the fairly limited items of food at their disposal.

The broth from beef and mutton should be used to pour over the bread, but after unsatisfactory experience with the broth of horse flesh I do not recommend its use in the same way. Horse flesh is best fed as steaks, roasted in front of the fire and then cut up in small pieces.

Beef and mutton are best boiled. The broth should be skimmed carefully during the cooking and the grease discarded. The broth is then suitable for soaking down the bread, and the meat, which should be chopped and never minced, added, together with a little jelly made from cow heels or sheep's trotters.

The consistency of the food is a matter for consideration. It should never be sticky or gummy. When mixed and ready to feed it should be just warm, and it should not adhere to the hand when thrust into it. The value of this test comes only from experience in doing it constantly and getting to know exactly if the food is right or wrong. Bread, if under-baked or not sufficiently stale, will invariably go gummy when hot broth or water is poured on, and I have found that a good way of preparing bread for the meal is to soak it down in cold water as follows :

Take an ordinary 2lb. loaf, cut it into quarters and

drop them into a bucket of cold water, placing something on top to keep them down? When the bread is thoroughly saturated with water, take each quarter out separately and squeeze it between both hands until no more water will exude. The bread will then crumble up beautifully and almost dry, and absolutely devoid of any suggestion of stickiness. The broth poured over this, with the meat added, makes the best of feeds. The jelly referred to above should not be mixed up with the food in bulk for the kennel in the mash-tub. The jelly should be added to each feed.

Cow heels can be purchased from the butcher dressed and ready for use, but many country butchers do not do this but will sell the set of heels for a few pence (a shilling at the outside for the set). Few people, however, know how to dress these articles, and a brief hint here may be of use to many.

To dress a cow heel, take water absolutely boiling and pour into a bucket or bath, and then take it just slightly off the boil by throwing in half to a pint of cold water. Next take the heel and thrust it into the water and keep it on the move by pushing it round and round for about a minute. Take it out and with the back of a knife, used as one would use a razor, going with the hair, the latter should come clear of the skin like slime. The whole success of the process depends upon the condition of the water. If it is right, you should dress a heel in three minutes from the time you put it into the water. If the water is not right and the hair gets set on through the hardening of the hide, nothing on earth will remove it. You may make a few mistakes at first, but you will hit the right idea soon. If you wish to remove the horn from the hoof, put the hoof into boiling water for a couple of minutes and insert the point of a meat-hook into it at the top and give a sharp pull. It comes off easily.

A sheep's head can be similarly treated, and if you are successful first of all in being able to get heads with the wool on and acquire the art of scalding them when you have got them, you will have heads which are heads and not skulls with an ounce or two of flesh. The best part of the head goes in the skinning. In Scotland, where the sheep's head is a dainty dish, they are prepared by singeing, the local blacksmith frequently doing the job. I have done cow heels by this method, but it is uncertain, for if left a few seconds too long in the fire, the skin hardens and the hair becomes immovably set on.

Sheep's head at all times is a change which the greyhound welcomes. The feed can be made most appetising. The broth, when thickened with rice, and all boiled to a cream with bread and broken up particles of flesh added, is one of the best feeds possible.

The best part of beef is from the hind-quarter. Bullock's throat makes a good change. This should be well boiled whole and given to the dog to munch.

If off condition and requiring light diet, tripe cooked in milk will be found beneficial, but there is not much in tripe upon which to do work. As to mutton, the best end of the neck or leg is the best. The former may be stewed or boiled and the latter boiled or roasted. Bones, I am certain, should be withheld when the dog is in strong work. Under ordinary conditions a dog should be given bones to gnaw, but looking to the large pieces which it is possible for a greyhound to bite off and swallow it is unsafe for him to make a course with its sudden twists and turns with sharp and jagged bones in his inside.

The best time to feed is in the afternoon between four and five o'clock.

As to water, it will be found that if the dog is properly fed, he will require very little to drink. The moisture required for his proper health should be contained in his food, and as milk is given daily while in training, there is little need for water. What water is given should be distilled. If after a run a greyhound manages to reach water and steals his fill, the work of the trainer is almost instantly undone. A dog with the squarest back imaginable will lose it in a single night after an inordinate drink of cold water. If in any way distressed, and water seems necessary, allow the dog two or three swallows and then wash his mouth out. In this way he will probably get a few trickles in addition, but the cooling effect of swilling out the mouth is all sufficient and achieves the same end in restoring the dog.

The system of feeding just described is applicable to the coursing dog but may be followed with confidence in training racers also. The only difference which it may be necessary to make will be with reference to quantity. The racing dog will never have to do the same amount of work, so that his ration may have to be reduced, but this cannot be done over a long period. If he is putting on fat, alter the proportion of flesh to bread and for the last few days fat can be got off by feeding toasted bread and strong jelly. Roughly speaking, the ration for the greyhound should be one half-ounce to every pound of his weight. Thus, a sixty-four pound dog will require two pounds of food per day. If this proves to be too much, consult food values and see that he is deriving the same muscle, nerve and blood-forming matter from his reduced diet. Before ever reducing the ration be sure that he is not suffering from too little work. It is, if he can stand it, always better to increase work than to decrease food.

## FOOD VALUES

Relative to Proteid (tissue former and force-producer) and Carbohydrate (temperature to body and energy required for vital and muscular action), as contained in :—

|  | PROTEID | CARBOHYDRATE |
|---|---|---|
| Cow's milk | contains 10 parts of the above | 30 parts of the above |
| Mutton (lean) | ,, 10 ,, ,, ,, ,, | 19 ,, ,, ,, ,, |
| Mutton (fat) | ,, 10 ,, ,, ,, ,, | 27 and upwards according to quality |
| Beef (lean) | ,, 10 ,, ,, ,, ,, | 17 parts of the above |
| Horseflesh (lean) | ,, 10 ,, ,, ,, ,, | 15 ,, ,, ,, ,, |
| Rabbit | ,, 10 ,, ,, ,, ,, | 2 to 5 ,, ,, ,, |
| Hare | ,, 10 ,, ,, ,, ,, | 2 to 5 ,, ,, ,, |
| Potatoes | ,, 10 ,, ,, ,, ,, | 90 ,, ,, ,, ,, |
| Barleymeal | ,, 10 ,, ,, ,, ,, | 57 ,, ,, ,, ,, |
| Wheatflour | ,, 10 ,, ,, ,, ,, | 46 ,, ,, ,, ,, |
| Oatmeal | ,, 10 ,, ,, ,, ,, | 50 ,, ,, ,, ,, |

## CHAPTER XII

### THE FORS AND AGAINSTS KEEPING GREYHOUNDS IN THE HOUSE

IN dealing with the training of greyhounds, it has been with reference to the kennel kept dog purely. When the number of dogs exceeds one or two it will be impossible to keep them in the house, but if not exceeding that number there are advantages in keeping them indoors, but these advantages, I greatly fear, ar eoutweighed by the disadvantages accruing to both owner and dogs equally.

Greyhounds, perhaps more than any other dogs, hanker after human companionship and doubtless undergo much heart-burning when confined to kennels, for most of them when at walk have been able to gratify the omnipresent desire for association with man. If admitted to the house when in training, they gain much through being made happy, which is probably the prime secret of successful training. Again, if in the house, a much closer watch can be kept on the dog's state of health from day to day, and this is particularly important on the actual day before his appearance in the field or on the track. If permitted to live in, it is a foregone conclusion that nowhere in the house will satisfy the grey-

H

hound as sleeping quarters, but his master's own bedroom. The disadvantage here will be with reference to the master only. However, taking the rough with the smooth, it can in many ways amount to an advantage on the part of the master. On the night before coursing or racing, when the dog is all ready and tuned up, it may happen that he is restless, it may be that he is thirsty, in which case the master must arise and administer drink, after which the dog will settle down to a night of restful slumber, always so necessary for success on the morrow. Other causes of restlessness which can be removed by a little timely attention will also be observed. Then, if the dog should groan in his sleep, or perhaps eject some of his food, it ought to be a direct intimation to the master that all is not well with the dog for his race or otherwise. Such indications of temporary slight unfitness, when the dog sleeps in the kennel, cannot be observed. To introduce a kennel dog to the house on the night before running is an unwise procedure. It is too much of a change, and the chances are that, even if perfectly well, he will not settle down in circumstances so greatly altered. The mistake has been made on very many occasions on nights preceding coursing meetings. Novice trainers, being either over-anxious as to the safety of their dogs or filled with too much kindness, elect to have the dog or dogs to sleep in their rooms, with the result that the dogs never settle down and by the morning are exhausted and out of temper, and as a consequence start the day dully instead of with the bounding energy which must be there if they are going to do any good.

A further great advantage of the house-dwelling greyhound is that he seldom or never suffers from skin trouble of any kind. Skin trouble, I am inclined to believe, is due very largely to dogs lying together. Dogs radiate great heat and stuffiness, and those two factors make for affections of the skin. The fact, too, that the dog in the house stands so much better chance of being fed on more carefully prepared food may have a good deal to do with the absence of skin trouble, for it is definitely known that some forms of the disease are due entirely to dietetic reasons.

The disadvantages of keeping greyhounds in the house are manifold—they are innumerable. To begin with, the dog does not have the same opportunities for rest as does the kennel dog. The chief reason for this is that he has no abiding city. If he has, it is a room set aside for himself in which he is not so restful as in the kennels, for, being with you and yet not with you in the house, he is eternally getting up to whine in order to attract your attention so that he may be allowed out. If, on the other hand, he is quiet, it is a moral certainty that the master will go to have a look at him and thus rouse him from the rest which he must take to train well. Then again, unless he is permitted to sleep on the bed of the master (which he is certain to monopolise, if given half a chance), the bed allotted to him is uncomfortable and not half so adapted to his needs as the kennel bench with high front and depth of straw. Straw cannot be thrown down in one's house, and there is no real substitute. An easy chair is greatly coveted by the greyhound, but in this he has to lie coiled up in a ring instead of sleeping outstretched, which he should do to be thoroughly healthy and relaxed. I have seen a greyhound reclining on a chesterfield, set apart for his entire use, but even this on winter nights when the fire has long since gone out and the temperature run down, is a poor substitute for the deep straw bed into which he can burrow and almost disappear. On the most luxurious of chesterfields a dog with a rug over him can lie and shiver. His feet get cold, and then his legs, and after that he begins to shake all over, and his only remedy is to get up and walk about, committing at the same time at least three indiscretions—tiring himself out, making a filthy mess and waking up the house. All these are detrimental to master and dog, for in the first instance the dog's health is affected and any chances of success; secondly, the carpet has suffered hurt, the dog also; and, thirdly, because the slumbers of the family have been disturbed, also the dog has probably to take the end of the lead across his ribs. His life indoors is not a happy one. If he must live in the house, for his sake and yours, make him comfortable at night. In addition to providing him with a sofa, he must have a blanket or eiderdown as well. This should be thrown right over him and well tucked in, when nothing further will be heard of our friend until the morning, but the drawback is that he is so very comfortable that after a time he does not want to get up at all.

The feeding question is another tremendous trouble in the house. The food prepared for the dog is better than that prepared in kennels for a number, but this is counterbalanced inasmuch as the dog is regarded as a dust bin and a convenient medium for getting rid of stray morsels of food not otherwise required. To keep him safe from this over-feeding, nothing short of continual muzzling is of the slightest use.

If he is not eating, he is drinking. Water is certainly essential to a dog but in great moderation, and to observe moderation in the house amounts practically to an impossibility.

Irregularity is of all the greatest disadvantage. No matter how carefully you arrange your plans, it takes great strength of mind to live up to them. " I will have him out at half-past seven to the minute," says the man who determines to train his dog from his house. " I will give him twenty minutes or so in the meadow to gallop about and empty himself and then home for a good rub down and a light breakfast. He can then have a good rest until eleven o'clock and after that have a couple of hours on the road. Home for a good dressing down with an afternoon's rest until his feed at five o'clock, after which he will be given another spin round the meadow and finish for the day, with the exception of the last few minutes in the garden before retiring." Alas ! How subject all those good resolutions are to the exigencies of life in the house. Half-past seven arrives, you are a little tired and remain in bed, or the morning is wet and the fag of walking to the meadow looks ominous in the extreme. " After breakfast will do," becomes the normal state of affairs. Meantime, the unhappy dog wanders about, knowing not what to do. He whines and whimpers and implores, getting on the nerves of all until he is shouted at and cowed into submission to his fate. The morning walk presently takes place with less and less regularity. The dog gets fat and then the work is taken up again with exaggerated severity when fatness gives way to stiffness. The feed which is timed for five is given at four if more convenient, or deferred until six for a similar reason. There is then no time for the after supper exercise, accidents take place in consequence, the sufferer being the poor dog. He either misbehaves or defers as long as he can the necessity to relieve nature, thereby getting himself into a thoroughly bad state of health. The end of the story is invariably the same. The dog is never got fit, and has in the end to be banished to kennels where he benefits from regularity but suffers through being taken away from human companionship which to him is heaven, and for the joys of which he can put up with much. There is a further great drawback to having a dog in the house, and that is the difficulty of giving medicine when required. In kennels, whenever this need becomes apparent, the physic is administered on the spot, but notwithstanding the fact that it may be perfectly obvious that it should be done, one thinks twice if the dog is in the house. The subsequent mess which one always must expect takes the uppermost place and one hopes that he may be better to-morrow and that the oil may not be necessary. In this way much valuable time may be lost and the ounce of oil which would have been all sufficient yesterday becomes a long vet's bill from to-day.

Then there is the question of the dog's mentality to be considered. For coursing purposes it is undesirable that the dog should become too intelligent. It is when he becomes so and uses his brain too much in circumventing the hare that his career as a coursing dog comes to an end. If continually with people, he is bound to become more intelligent than if kept in kennels, so from the coursing point of view this may be detrimental to him. With reference to racing, however, the opposite may be the case. Speed is certainly as essential on the track as in the field, but a brainy dog at the racing game can make up by the use of his head for some slight deficiency in speed.

The risk which the dog runs, too, in being taken out too often militates against his always being in that keen and alert state of mind which is required when wanted to course or race. If a dog is easy to hand in the house and some member of the family is going out on an errand there is ever the tendency to slip on the lead and take the dog along. This may be good for him in several ways, but it does not make " going-out " the novelty it is to the kennel dog. Just like humans, dogs get *blasé*, and this is the very last thing which a greyhound must do.

If from necessity or otherwise, therefore, you must keep your running dog in the house, the first thing to be done is to draw up a programme on rational lines of training and stick to it. Hang it up in your bedroom where you can see it, and in every room you use. Let it be where you never can forget it, and always remember that to carry out that programme is money to you and kindness to the dog. He will do his bit if you will do yours.

## CHAPTER XIII

### A GREYHOUND'S PROPER RACING WEIGHT

EVERY dog has his proper racing weight. Particular attention to this fact will have to come into the reckoning both by owners and racecourse executives if true form is to be maintained. Up to date, little or no attention has been bestowed upon the subject. Each track has had a couple of hundred greyhounds kennelled on the premises, comprising fat dogs and thin dogs and dogs in all stages of coming on or going off. From out of these races had to be made up, and all that was aimed at was to get six dogs together which could do the course in as nearly as possible the same time. Consequently, dogs losing fat for muscle and condition went up and dogs making fat and no muscle went down.

Weight, when it is the right weight, is the greatest guide to form, but weight, when not taken in combination with condition, is nothing. Coursing trainers knew the weights of their dogs, and this was not so easy to get at as it can be on the race track. The coursing man looked at his dog and by the aid of his hand could say at once if he were too big or too light. If too big, he knew approximately how much should come off, and, furthermore, he knew how to do it. If the dog looked too light he went the other way to work. When he got the particular animal to the weight which in his estimation was the right weight the dog was run. On occasions, although at the right estimated weight, the dog may have appeared to run badly, in which case he might revise his first opinion and allow him a little variation each way. Presently he discovered to a nicety what the running weight should be and could always work up or down to it.

The race track presents few difficulties as to ascertaining the proper racing weight than those encountered by the coursing trainer. It is at least much more easy to keep a racer at weight than a courser, because the racing dog runs prescribed distances, whereas it is never possible to know when the courser will get a long and gruelling course.

It should be within the province of every race track executive to decide first of all if a candidate for a race is in racing condition. To adjudicate on condition is no task for the novice. Only men who can claim truly to have had years of experience in training, and not only in training but successful training at that, should be put in the position to give their opinion on people's property. How to gauge condition is not a thing which can be learned from reading a manual on the subject. I do not propose, therefore, even to attempt to describe condition at this point. I would rather advocate most strongly that an official be appointed on every track who

is competent to say definitely if a dog is in running
condition before admitting him to a race. If he is
satisfied that the condition is right, the dog should be
officially weighed for further reference. It is as important that the dog's weight be published as his time and
the distance by which he won. On each occasion of
running the weighing should be repeated, and in this
case a dog's absolute running weight to the fraction
of an ounce should be ascertained. It may be a difficult
matter to carry out and may lead to many disputes,
but it should be further within the jurisdiction of race
track executives to refuse a dog, even if he turns the
scale at his proper weight, if in their opinion that
dog is carrying soft fat.

For obvious reasons a certain type of man may think
fit to let his dog down and bring him back to weight by
manipulation of the diet, losing muscle and gaining fat.
For instance, a dog's proper racing weight has been
ascertained clearly to be sixty-four pounds. He can be
taken away for a matter of three weeks, in which time
he can have undergone the process of being wasted down
to say five pounds under his running weight, and thereafter be brought back to sixty-four pounds by means
of lots of bread and very little flesh. When, however,
he attains sixty-four pounds in this way he will be an
almost unrecognisable animal. Instead of exhibiting
the back, off which we are wont to say " an egg would
not roll," his back will be sloping off on each side and

there will not be a glimpse of ribs. Taking the dog all round he will lack shape and animation. His coat, instead of being like satin, will be woolly and long.

Then there is the other way of going to work. Sixty-four pounds can be allowed to run up to sixty-nine or so by heavy meal feeding. During this process we are gaining fat and all the time losing muscle.

The thinning down process can then be accomplished by feeding meat only and witholding all farinaceous food, leaving the dog in as bad a plight as in the other case referred to above.

When the science of judging condition becomes known to more racing enthusiasts, it will be their greatest boon in racing their dogs. Open racing, which is bound to become the one form of racing, will make it important for owners training their dogs privately to become judges as to condition, so that they do not take them to tracks obviously without a chance of winning.

There is a somewhat widespread idea that a dog cannot be kept at weight for any great length of time, but with reference to the race track a dog can and has been proved to be able to stay at weight and keep fit for months on end. His right weight is his healthy weight, and a dog or a man or anything else cannot be better than in full health. It is the forced and artificial condition which does not last.

Regarding the right of an appointed official to adjudicate on condition, I have said that this may lead to many disputes. It will undoubtedly lead to high words, but if the official knows his job and is confident that the dog is not in condition if even at the right weight, a decision to satisfy all can be arrived at by putting him in the trap and giving him a trial round the track, when his time will tell the tale definitely.

A certain variation of weight must of course be allowed, but this should be limited to one pound over or the same amount under the weight previously struck as the dog's proper racing weight.

Slight as though this variation may be, it means something, so that if weights are published as well as times, the public have further form to go upon and probably the most exact form ever yet thought out.

When this time comes, which it must, and all dogs are classified according to weight as well as time, it should produce much better and fairer racing. While only time is taken into account, the big dog is always on the best terms. The small dogs get shouldered out at the bends, not being able to withstand the superior weight of the big ones. If weights are published it will then be optional for an owner entering dogs in open races to enter a small one amongst big ones if he cares, but, through having all information to hand, he will certainly be able to run him in what race seems to be the one in which he has the best chance.

The best proof of the inequality of small greyhounds when classed with bigger ones is the absolute prejudice there was and is against bitches on the tracks. The bitch is smaller than the dog, and, notwithstanding the fact that bitches have run in many races, very few have proved winners. Albeit that they were put in races where their times and those of the dogs were as nearly as possible the same, their smaller size was their handicap. Bitches have won, it is true, and " Beaded Biddy " even broke all records at Wembley, but she was a big bitch. Her weight is given as sixty-two pounds, which makes her as big and bigger than some of the dogs she met. The fact that she was outstanding is largely due to her size.

However, in the near future, when races will be advertised and the entries published in the same way as for horse races, an owner will engage his dogs in several races and decide in which to run him when he sees the list of entries.

Reverting to the matter of keeping a dog at weight over a period of time, the American experts on greyhound racing are of opinion that our system of feeding cooked meat to the greyhound is less conducive to the praticability of keeping a dog at weight than their system of feeding the meat raw. A leading authority on training greyhounds for the track in America says that he never gives his dogs cooked meat at any time of their training. The beef or mutton is cut up in small pieces and fed with sound biscuits or brown bread and cooked carrots. On this diet he claims to be able to keep a dog at weight for any length of time.

## CHAPTER XIV

### MODERN TRANSPORT AND ITS EFFECT ON COURSING

AT first sight it may appear difficult to conceive why modern transport by railway and motor-car can have affected coursing in the slightest degree, but a brief survey of how the matter stood prior to modern modes of getting about will show definitely that there is something in it.

When the only mode of locomotion was by coach, chaise or cart, people did not move about with the same facility as they do to-day and confined their perigrinations to a more or less narrowly prescribed area. In consequence, the sportsmen who followed the leash provided themselves with greyhounds suitable to the country in which they could follow the sport. Up until the days when the steam-engine opened up the country and made long-distance travel a possibility in greatly reduced time, the greyhounds of Great Britain were divided into five distinct families, each suited to the section of the country in which it lived.

These five varieties were Newmarket, Wiltshire, Lancashire, Yorkshire and Scottish.

The Newmarket dog prevailed in the Eastern Counties, and because of the geographical configuration of the country, where long runs-up were common, a greyhound of great size and speed was evolved. He was built for speed in the main, his powers for working ability being sacrificed. The Newmarket dog was flat-sided, but very deep in the chest, which afforded him ample heart and lung room, but he was, in addition, narrow-hipped and thus deficient in muscle attachment so that he seldom carried a back.

The Wiltshire dog, which operated in the county from which he took his name, Berkshire, Dorset, Hants and the Cotswold Hills, was the absolute antithesis of the Newmarket variety. He was a small, compact and very muscular animal, in weight not much more than thirty-five pounds. The Wiltshire dog had speed and close working qualities combined together with great stoutness, for he had strong, if short, running hares to follow. His conformation enabled him to stop suddenly, come round with the hare like lightning and shoot off again like the shot out of a gun. This Wiltshire family became heavily crossed with the Newmarket strain about the middle of the last century, and this was probably largely due again to modern methods of agriculture, whereby the open Downs over which coursing took place came extensively under cultivation; in a very short space of time this had the effect of greatly increasing the size and strength of the hares of the district.

The Lancashire family extended over the whole of the Midland area of England. In Lancashire a dog of

"Lickfinn Rover'; "Cheerful Joe"—"Ballynonty Black"), 1925 F.d., a general favourite at Wembley and a consistent winner of many races, familiarly known as "the poor man's friend." The property of Mr. and Mrs. Yokoyama.

"Ballynonty Jack" ("Little Jack"—"Ballynonty Black"), 1927 Bd.d. Although only 21 months old, this dog has already won many good races, and has gone through his first coursing season unbeaten. The property of Mr. and Mrs. Yokoyama.

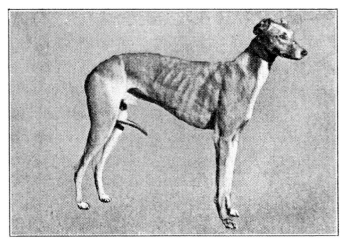

" Ruddy Bill " (" Jedderfield "—" Steam Whistle "), 1926 R.f.d., Clapton Stadium track record holder (33.80 sec. 550 yards flat). The property of Mr. A. Andrews.

Photo by]                                                                                    [Thos. Fall.
" Champion St. Blaise" ("Okeford Rascal"—" Butcher Girl"), 1911 W.bk.d., the most typical show dog of the present century. The property of Miss D. Beadon.

great height was essential, and to height and speed were sacrificed working qualities to perhaps a greater extent than in the Newmarket dog.

The nature of the country made it often impossible for the judge to ride, and as only the first part of the course could be under close observation, working quality and stoutness were altogether lost sight of, but the Lancashire dog is said to have been possessed of the latter in great quantity.

The Yorkshire greyhound, common to the northern counties of England, was a fast dog with considerable working ability, but deficient in stoutness, and, as a distinct family, was probably the first to disappear.

The Scottish dog was probably of English blood crossed with the old rough greyhound. There was no distinct type such as existed at Newmarket, in Wiltshire, Lancashire or Yorkshire.

There were many celebrated coursing families in Scotland and each maintained its own particular variety. It was only in characteristics that there was similarity. The Scottish dogs ran with great fire and determination, eager to kill but possessed of a little too much intellect, by virtue of which they too early in their career began to take liberties with their hares, ceasing to drive them with the determination which they invariably showed in puppyhood.

Each of these families was adapted to its own country, but of little use elsewhere, and this coursing men soon

I

began to realise when the day arrived on which a Scotch sportsman could remove his dogs for coursing at Newmarket with probably less difficulty than when he used to make the journey from Dumfries-shire to Lanark. Gradually, therefore, what was found lacking in one strain was acquired by a cross with the strain in which the quality required was dominant until a fixed type was reached. Even to-day we still have strains in which we know that speed predominates and in others working ability, so that with a knowledge of pedigrees and performances it is possible for the intelligent enthusiast to breed his greyhounds with a fair chance of producing winning stock.

The fixed greyhound type has carried another factor in coursing in its wake which further brings the sport in all parts of the country into terms of greater equality, and that is that coursing nowadays is run over country of very much the same character, but finishes up annually with the Waterloo Cup, run over ground of a different kind from most, which will test the all round quality of all the cracks of the season.

Speed is the main point for which the greyhound is now bred. Staying power is given much less attention than it was formerly. The coursing is on flat ground, much of it as smooth as a lawn, where everything depends upon the run-up. Even before we had the race track and the mechanical hare, we could have said with every good reason that coursing had given way to dog racing.

The speed of the greyhound to-day is without doubt
greatly improved to what it was, say, seventy to eighty
years ago.  There is no getting away from the fact if,
as we are told, courses of two and three miles were
common.  I question very much if under our modern
system of training our greyhounds could stay a course
of that extent, but when it is explained that greyhounds
when in training were asked for thirty miles a day it
will be readily understood that staying power was thought
more of than speed.  It cannot be argued either that
the hares were better hares in those days.  We know
they were not.

The Wiltshire hare at that time was a five pounder
as a rule, but there would be few hares in Wiltshire
to-day under eight pounds.

The scientific drainage of the land in Lancashire
has improved conditions for the hare as well as for every
other living animal, so that size and strength there also
have greatly increased.  Then there is the all important
factor in breeding known as " selection," and although
it is not generally realised, coursing in its up-to-date
form has done much to improve the type of the English
hare.  It would be a pity to pass by and not explain
how this has taken place.

Coursing clubs prefer to choose running ground
where hares are not too plentiful.  The reason for this
is obvious, but for the benefit of the novice it may be
better to explain that where hares exist in great numbers,

it is more difficult to drive a single hare past the slipper's box at a meeting, for when two or more hares are in evidence it is impossible to slip the dogs. If, too, there is an abundance of hares, there is always the danger of a fresh one jumping up after a course when the dogs are spent, and coursing, when in that condition, is certain to cause them grievous hurt. With apologies for this deviation from the subject, ground where there is just a fair hare population is much preferred to that whereon hares abound. It happens, therefore, that by continued wet and cold for weeks before an important meeting, that certain coursing grounds have become denuded absolutely of hares owing to the great speed of the greyhounds and the weakness of the hares. On such occasions the club concerned has found it necessary to re-stock the ground with hares. For this purpose, club servants make a journey to a part of the country where hares are to be found in great numbers in order to bring back, uninjured, enough to re-stock. The hares are taken in nets, and as a fairly high charge is made for live hares, the secretary of the club makes it his business to see that he is getting strong, large, young animals. In this way, therefore, by the system of careful selection, even the speed and staying power of the hares of the country has been improved. It is obvious that if the old greyhounds, which had to go a course of three miles at times, had to pursue the modern hare they would have to go a good deal farther than they used to. The old

mode of coursing was more akin to hunting than is the
style to-day.  We can take it as a fact almost, that the
hares are faster and stronger, and if our average course
is over in approximately the same time as a race over
525 yards on the track, there can be no doubt that our
present greyhound has the foot of the old.

Looking at it from whatever angle one cares, there
seems to be no doubt at all but that our greyhound has
improved in pace, muscular development, force of
nerve and working ability, on account of the best of all
the five families having been used in the making up of
the new dog.  Since the change took place, the advances
made by the press has also been a great factor in assisting
breeders to keep abreast of the times as regards the performances of greyhounds all over the country at meetings
both great and small.  A dog's career is now reported
from start to finish and a clear and reliable record
obtained, enabling those who do not visit many of the
meetings to form a correct opinion of any dog's true
worth.

I have no doubt that in the olden times it was a
great recommendation for a dog if he could be pointed
out and referred to as having coursed a hare for over
twenty minutes.  There are plenty of greyhounds to-
day which can do that, and it is frequently the boast
of some local sportsman, not up in public coursing,
that he has witnessed a course which lasted over half
an hour.  Probably such a statement is perfectly correct.

The dogs engaged in a journey of the kind would be for a certainty greyhounds with more or less entire freedom to run as they like and feed as they like. As a rule, having blood in them, they have the determination necessary and, having had plenty of food, if perhaps not of the right sort, have wind and strength but unable to exert that nervous energy which in a spurt can make their speed greater than that of the hare instead of being just about equal to it. This makes the ultimate issue depend upon the wearing-down system, and not the effort to go forward as our trained dogs do and either turn or kill within the space of half a minute.

I have seen a dog of the half-hour variety put into slips with a highly trained animal. The main issue on that occasion was that the untrained dog died. He was a well-bred dog, the property of a man who made himself a pest by shouting on all occasions the prowess of his dog and going so far as to say he could win the " Waterloo." A coursing man bet him a fiver that he would bring the slowest dog he possessed and beat the other's head off. It was a match at once, and I must say that the untrained dog must have been a good one had he been prepared. He at least made the effort to keep up with his rival, but it cost him his life.

Unlimited work makes for staying power, but it is the present method of walks of moderate length and hand gallops of moderate length which are the secret roads to a fast gallop after the hare. Speed to-day means all. We breed for speed and we feed for speed and train for speed. As I have already said, the level coursing grounds now almost universally in use make speed the chief factor, but although not called for on many occasions our present day dog could stay all day if required to do so. He cannot, however, be a sprinter and a long distance performer at the same time and under the same conditions. The amount of work done by a dog in training in days gone by, staggering to us, was done with a purpose. It was not only the distance he might have to course the hare which was considered, but how good he was behind the cart to reach a meeting. At one time it was the custom for coursing dogs to work their passage as it were to the coursing ground, frequently jogging along behind the carriage to a meeting more than a hundred miles from home. Railways and motor cars have put a stop to that and, incidentally, given us better dogs and better hares and, let us hope, sportsmen of equal quality to the men who did not mind making a journey of a hundred miles in wintry weather in an open cart to try their dogs. Would many of us risk it now ?

## CHAPTER XV

### BLOOD

" A DOG of the right blood " is an expression in daily use whenever greyhounds come under discussion. Now the question is, " What is blood ? What does it mean ? " It is certainly difficult of definition, and as actual blood plays no part in the qualities possessed by a dog entitling him to the supposed inheritance of the right kind of blood necessary in a flier, we must analyse the various attributes for success in the greyhound.

It was supposed at one time that the blood globules in a thoroughbred horse were of a different shape to those found in horses of other breeds, but the microscope has long since exploded that fallacious conclusion. Why the blood was concluded to have something to do with the necessary qualities for speed and staying power in the horse was doubtless due to the fact that, in the main, highbred horses are possessed of thin and delicate skins through which the blood vessels show up clearly. This circumstance undoubtedly suggested to the minds of the ancients that it was blood that counted and nothing else. Even to this day we are wont to say with reference to man, horse and dog, " Blood will tell." Take it as you will, in the blood of

the duke and the navvy, of the racehorse and the cart
horse, the greyhound and the lurcher, according to
which ever species of the genus animal they belong to,
no difference can be found. In the highbred horse or
greyhound, however, there is one little difference not
unconnected with blood which is worthy of note. The
vessels which carry the blood, so apparent to the eye
from beneath the skin, are more numerous than in
animals of less delicate composition, such as the cart
horse. Being more numerous, these vessels are capable
of containing more blood, so that during the very
severe struggles of a long and sustained gallop, the heart
and lungs are revived from the overwhelming quantity
of fluid, which would otherwise be dangerous to the
safety of the animal.

It is, however, in the brain and nervous system that
the great difference lies. That which is termed " Good
Blood " is dependent therefore on the brain and nervous
system.

A racehorse, on that assumption, requires to be
possessed of a brain of a character which will enable
him to have quickness and cleverness in the stroke of
his gallop. The most perfectly made thoroughbred in
external form, without the proper formation of brain
and nervous system to control his bodily actions, will
undoubtedly be an animal altogether deficient in the
two qualities essential to make him a successful racer,
namely, speed and stamina. These same qualities

are as requisite in the greyhound as in the racehorse, but, in addition, there are other qualities necessary to his work of coursing the hare. These further qualities should be four in number. They are tact, destructiveness, jealousy, and a total disregard of injury. A greyhound with a brain in which these qualities are developed strongly, even though of comparatively poor frame, will beat an animal of the most approved make and shape deficient in the qualities just referred to, provided always that in addition the former has the requisite nervous system to enable the various organs to make the effort dictated by the brain.

Tact, we will take to mean the quality in the dog to command himself at his turns. That is, when the hare comes sharply round he should come round with her with niceness of perception, not overshooting the mark as he will do if not possessing the necessary quality of brain to command him at the turn.

The quality of destructiveness is the instinct and desire to kill and to impel him forward in his work to seize his quarry.

Jealousy he must possess in a marked degree to keep him either in possession of his game or to seize possession of it from his rival.

Disregard to injury is necessary to enable him to continue in the course with unflagging fire even when hurt, fatigued or with his game hopelessly beyond his grasp.

A dog possessed of these various qualities is termed a " dog of blood," but it will be obvious from the foregoing remarks that what stamps a dog a good one is due to the brain and the nervous system. Going further, we may assume that what is usually referred to as "blood," is a high state of perfection or condition of all the organs of the body depending upon the development of brain and nervous system, and requiring the brain to be large in the part where resides any particular quality desirable. The bulldog, whose animal instincts are developed abnormally in proportion to his intelligence, is wide across the ears as compared with the measurement behind the eyes, showing that the animal instincts are resident in the posterior of the brain and the intellect in the anterior portion. The poodle is held as being the dog of greatest intelligence. His head is of uniform measurement across the ears and behind the eyes.

The coursing greyhound in whom we require destructiveness, jealousy and disregard to injury should therefore be wider between the ears than behind the eyes, the three qualities in question being dependent upon the development of the posterior portion of the brain. No great degree of intelligence is necessary, or in fact desirable, in the coursing greyhound. The continuance of his running career beyond two or three seasons will depend as much or even more upon the development of his faculties than on his general fitness in wind and body. When intelligence (running cunning) makes its appearance, it means that jealousy has been given up. He no longer drives his hare with the fire bred of jealousy, but runs slack, allowing his rival to do the work in order that by departing from the rules of the game he can kill without exerting himself to any great extent.

Blood we have considered so far with reference to coursing only, but it would appear that what may be termed good blood from the coursing point of view may not be good blood from the point of view of racing.

Tact, if taken to mean the quality in the dog to command himself at the turns, need not be present in the racing dog. As compared with the sharpness of the turns in coursing, the bends on the track are not worthy of the name, and as an illustration of what I mean to convey, I am going to take " Grouse " as an instance of a greyhound which, deficient in tact, was a coursing failure, yet a racing success. " Grouse," at his turns, had the defect of cutting all over the place. He was utterly unable to steady himself, but the lack of the quality of being able to do so did not affect him adversely upon the track. Tact was the only one of the four qualities missing in " Grouse." He had the destructive spirit in a high degree developed in him, he was jealous and did not know fatigue. He also possessed plenty of pace and stamina.

The second quality (destructiveness) is as essential in the racer as in the courser, for without it I do not believe that dogs run as well. Racing dogs, I am convinced, know as well as you do that the mechanical hare is a fraud, but nevertheless they are quite prepared to tear it in ribbons if they can catch it.

When, on occasions, through defects in the mechanism the hare has stopped, the greyhounds have made short work of it. Unless a dog has killed a hare, he is not likely to chase the mechanical hare with the same fire as he otherwise would do. A dog in whom the quality of destructiveness is not strongly developed will show even less keenness for the mechanical hare.

With reference to jealousy, we are now touching on a quality which, in the racing dog, can be dispensed with to advantage. Jealousy keeps a dog to his game, so that the dog which sticks to his game on the track, unless possessed of phenomenal speed, is always less likely to win than an unjealous dog which makes for the inside, thereby reaching the winning post in a much shorter distance than the jealous dog plodding round with his nose behind the hare on the outside. We have considered " Grouse " as an instance of the dog devoid of tact, and as the converse case we are now going to consider " General Service," a dog which in the coursing field was eminently successful although he just missed being great. On the race track he has been a failure, and unless he can develop intelligence and substitute it for jealousy, he is ever likely to remain a failure. " General Service " has speed, tact, destructiveness and jealousy all highly developed in his character, and he was, on all his occasions of running, trained to the minute. What the particular defect in his make-up was, does not matter materially perhaps to the present question, but it was probably that he lacked a disregard for disappointment.

" General Service " is one of those dogs who will stick to his game. He has been beaten time and again by dogs who have not got his pace or determination, but to whom he has gone down by virtue only of travelling the longer distance, so jealous is he of the others that he must keep close to his game from start to finish.

As matters stand at present on the race track, so far as desired qualities in the greyhound are concerned, in addition to speed there would appear to be three requisites only, viz.: Destructiveness, tact and a fine disregard for disappointment. In case, however, that I may cause confusion as to tact, which I pointed out was lacking in " Grouse " in the field but did not militate against him on the track, it will be necessary to investigate the term " Tact," and make it applicable to the requirements of a successful racing dog.

Destructiveness need not be dealt with as the meaning will remain the same.

Tact, in the strict sense of the word means, " Doing the right thing at a given time." When the hare turns in the course, and the greyhound turns also, absolutely in command of himself, in less than his own length, he is, according to rules, doing the right thing at the right time. Now, coming to the race track, where no such tactic is required and where the only opportunity for cleverness occurs in manœuvring for the rails, let us say that the dog with that proclivity is possessed of the tact required in so far as the track is concerned. In racing there can be no question of overtaking or catching the hare, and the one thing looked for is the capacity of the dog to get first past the post. That being so, the dog which has himself sufficiently under command to carry out his intelligent conception of getting the rails to shorten his journey must be credited with the possession of tact.

Now, coming to the third requisite in a racing dog, a fine disregard for disappointment will have to be developed in a markedly high degree, for if the mechanical hare is of any significance to the dogs their efforts to capture her will be marred by failure on every occasion upon which the mechanism behaves as the public would have it do. If, however, the mechanical hare is disregarded by the dogs and their sole object in extending themselves is to pass all others in front, we again come back to the quality of jealousy, but here again it will savour of a different character to the jealousy required in the coursing dog. At the risk of repetition, we took jealousy in the coursing dog to mean determination on the part of one competitor to keep possession of the hare, or, on the part of the other, to wrest it from him.

Reverting to the track, however, jealousy will be confined to the desire on the part of dogs ahead, to keep ahead, or those behind to pass the leader. It is highly probable, however, that this kind of jealousy is absent and the desire uppermost in the mind of the dog, in an inconsidered kind of form, is to overtake the hare even if he resorts to subterfuge to do so, that subterfuge being the tact to take the rails in order that he may not have to travel so far to accomplish his purpose. We could now go on to a long discourse on dog mentality, but that I fear would be serving no useful purpose, as the dog not being possessed of the faculty of speech we can only surmise how he thinks, without being able to learn from him in words how he really does it.

There is little doubt but that the greyhound gallops purely for galloping's sake, and when he is fit and well it takes little to induce him to do so. Even when not sent to exercise with another, a single greyhound in a field will go for all he is worth, simply out of sheer ecstasy of spirit and the joy of bringing into play the whole of his active organisation. Seeing others ahead only serves to make him extend himself the more, and he may pass the other without there being any fixed intention in his mind of doing so. We must therefore leave it at that and limit the chief attributes for success in a racing greyhound to the possession of the quality for destructiveness, tact and disregard for disappointment. Disregard of injuries and fatigue should not be of any consideration so far as the track is concerned, for the risk of accident is practically nil as compared with that in coursing, and even a seven hundred yards race should be a flea-bite to a greyhound in a moderate state of condition.

On this assumption, the animal passions of the racing dog will be less in evidence than the qualities of intelligence and a fine fortitude against disappointment, from which we may conclude that the head of a typical racer will differ in shape considerably from that of the ideal courser. There will be in the racer less difference in measurement between the ears and behind the eyes than that found in the coursing dog. In other words, the anterior portion of the brain will be more highly developed in the racer than in the courser, and the posterior portion of the brain will be of less development than in the courser.

If this assumption be correct, it brings us to a most interesting conclusion, which is, that coursing will always be coursing and racing will be quite distinct. The perfect coursing dog, up to the form of a Waterloo Cup winner, if put on the track and sticking religiously to the rules which would govern him in coursing, would probably beat all comers on the track owing their success to getting the inside and thereby making up for the lack of pace, but if the entrants are to be confined to moderate dogs of just average pace the dog possessing the jealousy requisite in the courser and sticking to it is going to

K

be beaten always by slower but more tactful dogs; " tact-ful " always being construed, as we have prescribed it should be, with reference to racing.

There is little probability that the really high-class coursing dogs will find their way to the tracks in any great number. The honest, moderate dog from the coursing field will ultimately be discarded by the racing owner as not being fast enough to carry on his honest intentions in face of the dishonest if more intel-ligent running of others, so that in the end a completely new family with racing merits will come into being, and will be bred from with the same care as is observed in the breeding of first-class coursers.

The time is already in view when a particular racing dog (or rather racing dogs), will be pointed out and refer-red to as " Being of the right blood." Just as tact will carry a different interpretation as applied to coursing or racing, so will the term blood with reference to each form of sport.

We have reviewed the five families of greyhounds which existed in the days before railway and mechanical transport facilities, which I say came to an end with these modern inventions, but we are rapidly approach-ing an era in greyhound history when one at least of the old types will be reverted to, and that will be to something very much on the lines of the Newmarket dog, characterised by size, pace and moderate stamina, but lacking any great degree of working ability. Great size in the dogs for the track is unnecessary, dogs of over seventy pounds are not to be preferred to dogs of the most useful average weight of sixty-four pounds. Bitches, however, of considerably over the average weight (say fifty-two to fifty-four pounds) are to be welcomed, because the bigger they are the nearer do they approach the dogs in a sport where speed means everything. Without any intention of labouring the point, it must be understood that in the big bitch there must of a necessity be more than her size present. She must be possessed of all the racing qualities. This being so, a sixty-two pound bitch is bound to stand more chance when pitted against average weight dogs than is a bitch of the average weight. The brilliant " Beaded Biddy " owed much of her success to her great size of sixty-two pounds.

To sum up, you cannot be sure that two greyhounds of equally good-looking external form will be equal in performances. One may be good, the other bad. On the other hand two greyhounds as dissimilar in appearance as a cart horse to a racehorse may hold a surprise, the inferior looking dog running the other pointless in all respects, and earning for himself the reputation of being the right " blood," which means only that brain and nervous system have made up adequately for his shortcomings as regards his common-looking frame.

# CHAPTER XVI

### SELECTION OF THE RACING BROOD BITCH

I HAVE already treated of the inequality of the average sized bitch to compete with the average sized dog on fair terms on the race track, where everything depends upon speed and the cleverness of dogs in which reside the intelligence to get the rails and shorten the journey, and have pointed out the enhanced chances of success which are possessed by bitches over the average size, upon the ground that they, provided they have plenty of speed, get on better terms of equality with the dogs. So far, these big bitches have been chance finds, but there is no guarantee that they are going to produce big bitches when retired to the stud. On the contrary, as many of them are themselves by smallish dogs out of similarly sized bitches, owing their increased size to some accident of feeding, etc., they are almost sure to throw smallish stock, as experience goes to prove that the progeny is as likely to resemble the family in greater measure than the parents. We therefore become confronted with a very difficult problem, namely, how to breed bitches of size to compete on terms of comparative equality with the dogs.

We cannot very well increase the size of the bitches

all round without increasing the size of the dogs also. If we do this, we are where we were. There will be cropping up from time to time in the future, as in the past, bitches of over the average weight, and this will apply to racing bred animals as well as to coursers. As indicated, feeding during the growing period influences size. If young and growing greyhounds are heavily flesh fed, with little or no farinaceous additions to the diet, the result will be big, overgrown, muscular animals with defective circulatory systems, that is, heart and lungs. By so feeding, the object might be achieved of producing large bitches, but it would be unwise to take bitches so produced as brood bitches, for unless they were by parents of more than average size they would not perpetuate size, but would in all probability hand down to their offsprings their bad circulatory systems.

As, however, the aim and object of the racing breeder is to produce racing greyhounds, dogs and bitches, and not bitches alone, it will be more profitable to pass on to the subject proper, and map out a clear scheme for selecting bitches which will produce first-class racers of both sexes, amongst which there is always certain to be a sprinkling of big bitches by accident, to say nothing of small dogs.

Now to come down to bedrock, we want to find in our brood bitches all the essential attributes of the racer. These attributes will be three in number. The first is speed; the second cleverness or tact, as applied to what the term stands for in the racing dog; and a sufficiency of the destructive instinct third.

Speed, when combined with great size as in the case of the old Newmarket family of greyhounds, gives us dogs which are not such close workers as the smaller and thick-set animals. But, as has already been pointed out, the working qualities of the greyhound are not called into requisition on the race track. We can therefore without fear take as a brood a big speedy bitch, even if her working qualities are nil. We ought to know, however, that she possesses the desire to kill, which is to say, the attribute of destructiveness. Being big and fast the chances are that she lacks jealousy, bringing into play in its stead the proclivity of allowing her rival to knock the hare about, depending upon her superior speed to kill just when she wants to toward the end of the course. In coursing this is called " running cunning," but for the requirements of the track we have called it " tact." What is cunning in coursing, is tact on the track. For coursing purposes, to breed on these lines would be almost sufficient grounds to warrant a man being certified insane, but coursing and racing are two absolutely distinct games, calling for entirely different attributes. Although we have to go in opposite directions to get the individual types for each, it is from the experience gained in breeding coursing greyhounds that the only data is available for breeding racers.

In addition to the four attributes : speed, destructiveness, cleverness and disregard of disappointment (the three latter of which are due to brain development and nervous system, and the first to nervous system only), with or without external perfection, consideration must be given to the health of the animal and also as to whether or not she has suffered any injury in training or during her running career. Furthermore, the family from which she comes must be looked up and the characteristics of not only sire and dam exhaustively examined, but also those of the grand-parents and great-grandparents if necessary. At the present moment there are no such records available for investigation, as there are no racing greyhounds as yet with racing parents, so far as the track is concerned. But of course there are some with parents in the coursing fraternity which virtually are or were racers, had there been race tracks where they could have demonstrated, but from what we have already learned about racing we can judge pretty nearly by looking up the performances of the antecedents of racing bitches, their weaknesses and strong points.

It is passing strange that two men, one a coursing enthusiast and the other a racing devotee, when looking at the same pedigree, could be the one condemning and the other appraising the same characteristic. The racing man for his purpose wants an animal with cleverness to get the rails, and will remark with satisfaction in reading up the performances of a forebear, " Yes ! he was a clever intelligent dog, for he let his rival do the work and when he had knocked the hare about the other just slipped in and killed." The coursing man, looking at the same details, will say with reference to the same animal, " No ! I can't have him, he was a thief and probably his sire was a thief." He could put it in other words and say, instead of calling him a thief, that he had too much intelligence to satisfy the rules of coursing or, putting it technically, could assert that the anterior portion of the brain was too highly developed. It is possible, therefore, to glean from coursing records how much speed, intelligence, destructiveness or stoutness was possessed by any given greyhound in the last half century at least. The term " stoutness " I mentioned in my last sentence advisedly. Stoutness in the full sense of the term is not required in the racing greyhound, but a factor which goes to make up stoutness is necessary, that being " disregard of disappointment." The two other main factors which constitute what is called stoutness are a disregard to fatigue and to injury.

I am not prepared to go so far as to say that there is no danger in the way of injury or fatigue on the track, but, compared with what has to be negotiated in the coursing field in those directions, it is negligible. Neither do I say that stoutness is not desirable on the track, but what I do mean to convey is that disappointment being omnipresent at the end of each race on the track and a disregard thereof the essential factor of stoutness in a racer, it is not altogether necessary that the two other factors should be possessed in any great degree. Risk of injury on the track, either from strain or falling on uneven ground at the turn, is practically a minus quantity and can be dismissed, while fatigue, unless a very artificial greyhound is going to be evolved or the present distances of races greatly increased, is a factor which also need not be considered.

A bitch which in the coursing field can go up to her hare with dash and fire, put in a few exchanges and then show slight fatigue, need not be turned down as a good brood bitch for breeding racers.

If you have to go to the coursing field to find your bitch for breeding racers, let your choice be for one of "blood," consistent with what is necessary for the track. If you can see her run, so much the better. Watch her pace and see how she comports herself to the trial. So far as pace goes, you and the coursing man will both admire the same quality, but if the bitch should lurch, thus showing too much intelligence, he will condemn while you praise. Again, if at the turn she should be unable to command herself with precision, although the coursing man will shrug his shoulders in disapproval, you, on the contrary, will be in no wise cast down, and later, if in the work the bitch upon which you have set your mind should be guilty of wide working, or exhibiting slight fatigue, it need in no way whatsoever put you off your fancy.

Having got a bitch with pace, brains, destructiveness and disregard to disappointment, you will have little difficulty in getting from her stock like herself or even better, for it is a fairly simple matter to improve pace, which we have decided is the chief attribute of the racing greyhound.

The bitch we have considered up to the present is the ideal racing type, perfect in everything external and possessing speed and all the other attributes. But it will not be possible at all times to pick up a perfect bitch, and in the majority of cases breeders will have to be satisfied with bitches in which all the attributes are not present.

Taking pace first : If this be lacking, it is due to the formation of the animal. She will as a rule be found to be thick-set, very compact and probably heavy in shoulder and too wide in the barrel to admit of easy action in the forelegs. If in this bitch you can discern intelligence, destructiveness and disregard of disappointment, and on examination of her family you find that it is on the whole gifted with speed, there is no reason why the slow bitch now under consideration should not breed you speedy racers. A very careful choice of sire will be necessary. Whatever fault the bitch has must not be present in the sire. Such a bitch as we have under discussion, if mated to a sire who was perfect in all respects except his shoulders, which we will suppose are heavy also, would of a certainty throw stock with accentuatedly heavy shoulders. Notwithstanding the fact that they might be improved in every other detail this would militate against their ever possessing pace, no matter how carefully reared and trained. In short, choose a dog whose strong points are the bitch's weak points and in other respects let his characteristics be at least equal to hers.

Regarding intelligence : This will be more difficult to acquire in greater measure in the stock than is possessed by the bitch. Fortunately, the greyhound is not a stupid dog ; on the contrary he is naturally intelligent but kept stupid artificially in order, as has already been pointed out, he may not learn to " run cunning." Intelligence is dependent upon the brain entirely and is confined to the anterior portion, but a lack of intelligence is only too often hereditary. It would take so much time to improve intelligence that as there are so many intelligent greyhounds to choose from it would be a virtual waste of time to try and improve it by the choice of a sire for a stupid bitch. What would be difficult of accomplishment in improving intelligence can be got at in another way by still further improving pace, but, personally, I would not breed from a bitch not sound in the head. There are as many mental deficients and degenerates amongst greyhounds as there are amongst humans, and experience goes to prove that whatever it be, man or greyhound, bad traits are much more easy to perpetuate and more difficult to improve than are the good qualities.

Destructiveness is an animal passion and dependent upon the posterior portion of the brain, and more easy of cultivation than is intelligence. The animal passions in dog and man are difficult to suppress and the killing instinct is still strong in us. If, therefore, your bitch is good in other respects but somewhat lacking in destructiveness it is a point easy of remedy, for there will be plenty of dogs available particularly gifted this way.

Now regarding the bitch which feels disappointments : This is a somewhat difficult point to advise upon as to its rectification in the bitche's stock. Regard or disregard for disappointment is dependent upon the nervous system. Disappointment affects different animals in different ways. Some are positively discouraged and just give up and are said to have no inclination for racing ; neither have they, but greyhounds of this type present a great problem in this way. I am not at all sure that the fault of giving up after a few experiences of the futility of catching the hare is not due to super-intelligence and not to faint heart or any other cause.

Greyhounds of a serious turn of mind, seeing that a fraud is being worked upon them, in my estimation, say to themselves that, it being quite obvious that the hare disappeared down a hole and shut a door on itself into the bargain, the fag of going all out to the end of the race is only so much wasted energy. There have been many instances of really speedy greyhounds which refused absolutely to do their best after the home bend, and most exasperating animals they are. They will go out and lead the field and, having got it beaten, they simply stop gradually and let the others pass with a sort of a " I-passed-you-all-any-way " expression. Not being sure if conduct such as this is due to an excess of intelligence or a lack of nerve, a bitch in which the fault is strong is a difficult subject as regards the choice of a sire who will counteract the evil. I think that the sire necessary will have to be chosen from what I like to call the light and airy brigade, which I am going to review now with reference to our brood bitch.

We have considered the bitch who just gives up the struggle when her chances look most rosy, and we have decided that she gives up for one of two reasons, either that she is too intelligent or is lacking something in nerve.

There is another type which has experienced disappointment but has overcome it and races on to the bitter end in a light and airy manner, taking little or no notice of the hare whatsoever. This type would probably go round as well if no hare were present, for in such a case the hare can be regarded only as a pace maker. It is only at the finish that this kind of greyhound realises that a capture would be pleasant and is as likely as not to lay hold of one of the other competitors in the race. These, I think, are the born racers and surpass in excellence, from the racing point of view, those greyhounds which go doggedly on race after race, month in and month out, pursuing honestly an object which they will never overtake. These greyhounds have of course the disregard for disappointment most strong in them, but I think as a sire for the " giving up " type of bitch I would rather use a dog from amongst the light-hearted fraternity, for they have no outward sign whereby we can say that they are disappointed even if they pretended they are not. If they are pretending, then all the more reason why we should make an endeavour to instil into the faint-hearted lady this estimable quality.

There is, however, a more certain and more satisfactory solution of the problem as to how this bitch should be bred, and that is by putting her to a coursing dog, noted for his disregard of disappointment. There can be no two ways as to the intentions of the coursing dog, whether he be a sticker or otherwise. It will be, for many a long year to come, to the coursing dog that the racing man will have to send his bitch, for it will be amongst the fashionable sires of the coursing field that will be found the maximum of speed and all the other attributes with the exception, perhaps, of intelligence— and that too will be there, requiring only to be developed.

There is nothing, however, against the choice of

a racing sire for a racing bitch, except at the present time there is nothing outstanding in the track which cannot be easily surpassed in breeding and everything else by most of the public sires now advertised at stud continuously. As time goes on, the choice of a sire from among the racing dogs will be presented with less difficulty than at present, as we do not know clearly yet what constitutes a racing dog. In purchasing a bitch from the race track for breeding purposes, when we look up her family, it is at present a coursing family which will come under observation, but in a few years, when the National Greyhound Racing Club's stud book has run into several volumes, it will be possible to say then what are the characteristics to look for in the sire.

As far as the bitch is concerned, her progeny is more likely to take after the characteristics of the family than of the peculiar properties of the bitch herself, and in selecting a brood bitch this is a fact not to be overlooked.

## CHAPTER XVII

### DISTEMPER

THIS, the greatest scourge with which dog owners are besieged, has baffled the medical and veterinary professions ever since it made its appearance; notwithstanding the many thousands of pounds which are expended annually on research work the identifying of the germ seems to be as far off as ever.

It was at one time considered to be typhoid fever and in its symptoms it is closely akin to that disease, but more recently it has been identified with greater accuracy with influenza.

There would appear to be little doubt but that is what it is. It comes in waves to our kennels in exactly the same way that influenza devastates humanity, and in 1918, when the country was held in the grasp of the worst attack of influenza known to history, when in many districts people died off like flies, distemper was at the same time raging and killing off dogs by the thousand. Mr. Gillard, since deceased, an eminent vet. at Oxford, and a specialist in dog diseases, told me at that time that he was convinced beyond all doubt that in the form in which influenza came that year, it was communicable from dog to man and vice versa, being called influenza in the man and distemper in the dog. Be that

Photo by]                                        [Bert Cooper.

"Graccola" ("Cocoanut V"—"Careless Lassie"), 1925 Bk.d., a brilliant
performer at Wembley, White City and Harringay on the flat and over
hurdles. Winner of 14 firsts, 7 seconds and three thirds. The property of
Mr. J. H. B. Gibbons.

Photo by]                                        [Bert Cooper.

"March Ahead" ("Beaded Dick"—"Mystery Gift"), 1926 Bd.d., the
"coming champion," having won in a short time three firsts
and four seconds on the flat and over hurdles. The property of
Mr. J. H. B. Gibbons.

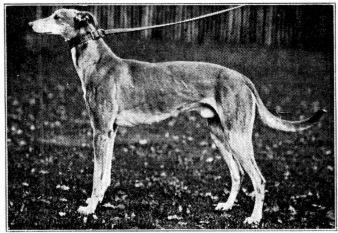

" Knavish Speed " (" Cheerful Speed "—" Dainty Dish "), 1924 F.d., winner of ten races at Wimbledon and the only dog to have won two 650 yards races. He appears an ideal sire for racing bitches. The property of Messrs. Cave and Bayntun.

" Horace " of Wembley. The mechanical hare trolley at Wembley Stadium. It weighs 27 cwt. and can attain a speed of 55 m.p.h

as it may, Mr. Gillard had a first-class opportunity of putting his theory to the test, for Oxford was the town where the influenza did its deadliest work. We hear a good deal nowadays of a disease called Gastric Influenza, but this I am certain is only an extra name for a particularly contagious form of distemper.

When distemper comes, it comes in all forms with certain common symptoms, so that if we are to call the form which attacks the stomach by a name different from distemper, we should at the same time invent new names for the forms which attack the lungs, the brain, and the nervous system. No germ having been yet discovered it is almost futile to think of the various vaccines, both prophylactic and curative, which are now upon the market, for there is no logical ground upon which any one of those can be offered as a cure for distemper. It is only when the day comes and a germ is isolated that the necessary vaccine can be prepared. It may even be that each form of distemper has its own particular germ, in which case the matter becomes more complex than ever.

An eminent veterinary informs me that he has derived great benefit by having a culture prepared from a dog's own discharge and then injecting him with it. However, I have had wonderful luck in bringing dogs through distemper without any injection whatsoever, but, had I used one, I would no doubt be of opinion that the cure was due to its properties.

L

" That which cannot be cured, must be endured,"
and distemper is a case in point. You cannot cure distemper. You can merely nurse it, and how best to set
about that disheartening task is a hard thing to say.
Personally, I believe that the great majority of the
deaths in distemper are due to forcing the dog to eat
when he is least inclined to do so. My methods may
be Spartan, but I am certain that they are rational.

Let us consider the first symptoms of distemper.
The dog refuses food. He is lethargic and heavy-eyed.
There are other reasons beyond on-coming distemper
which will induce a dog to refuse his food, but whatever
the reason may be, the obvious thing to do is to administer medicine, and an emetic is the nearest cut to the
accomplishment of the object. Vomiting is a natural
act in the dog, but repeated vomiting is a certain sign
that something radically wrong is taking place.

However, if the emetic is administered as soon as
the dog looks dull and refuses food, it is possible that an
attack of distemper may have been cut in the bud.
Many old hands use common table salt in the proportion
of, say, two teaspoons to a wineglassful of water. This
has the immediate effect of making the dog vomit,
and it frequently at the same time acts upon the bowels
in an incredibly short space of time. I know for a
certainty that I have cut many attacks of distemper
short in this way.

Another splendid emetic is common soda : the

ordinary household variety which is used in cooking cabbage or in the work of washing clothes. In ordinary cases, not distemper, soda is excellent for emptying the stomach of a burden which it cannot throw off by itself, but in the first symptoms of distemper I believe that, in addition to making the dog throw off the mucous matter and catarrh, it has at the same time some valuable antiseptic effect on the various organs with which it comes into contact.

If, however, the first symptoms should have escaped notice, the next thing is that the dog becomes very rapidly weak and loses flesh, and by the end of seven days, from the time when the trouble began, is a mere shadow of his former self. A dry husky cough will set in and there is pretty certain to be discharge from eyes and nose. By this time it will be quite apparent, even to the man of small experience, that distemper is present and it is time to be getting busy.

The patient should be isolated in a dry kennel free from draught. Heat beyond that to which he has been accustomed is unnecessary, but it is essential that he be given ample fresh straw in which to curl up. His temperature should be taken, and if found to be over normal to any alarming degree, it should be reduced at once. To keep the bowels open and the temperature down are the two most important things which can be done for a dog in distemper. Aspirin is a drug with the most beneficial effect on dogs. In the event of high temperature a greyhound may be given two or three tablets with every safety. If in twenty minutes it is found that the temperature has not been reduced, give more aspirin and, without forcing the patient too much, administer an ounce dose of castor oil, syrup of buckthorn and syrup of poppies in equal parts. From experience gained, I am convinced that this is the best of all treatments for distemper.

The second week may be termed the exhaustion period. It is also the most dangerous. The greyhound is a highly strung animal, and although possessed of all the attributes which we have reviewed, under severe and exhausting illness, his nerve breaks down and he is only too prone to make up his mind that he is going to die. In fact, I believe that many greyhounds elect to die, and do it. A little human comfort and encouragement during the exhaustion period goes, I think, considerably further than food. Food of the right kind should be offered to the patient frequently, but after a long experience I have come to the conclusion that it is useless to drench him if he will not feed of his own free will. It would appear to be absolutely inhuman to let any animal lie and apparently die for want of food, but yet, on the other hand, you may be killing him by drenching him at the wrong time. It is a difficult problem and one fairly bristling with the fors and againsts, but my principle now is to offer the food from time to time and, contrary to all the rules and regulations laid down for dogs in health, leave the food down with the dog when he is alone. Not long enough, of course, for it to get sour or stale. It is remarkable how many cures I have had through adopting this plan. There are just the right moments when the patient feels like a mouthful, and if left to himself will help himself; a couple of laps taken in the natural way is worth a pint put down him as a drench. When the temperature is up he will be disinclined to eat, but there are times when he will get a certain amount of relief by the temperature going down, and it is at those junctures that he will arouse himself and, feeling slightly better, will take a little nourishment. Drenching invariably produces vomiting, and when a dog is down and out and with but merely sufficient strength to walk a few steps at the best of times, he will be unable to stand when seized with a paroxysm of vomiting, and will lie where he is and befoul his legs and feet. It is at this point that he loses heart entirely and refuses to make any further effort. He seems to lose all interest in himself and just gives up the ghost. It is a strange thing, but I have observed it on so many occasions that I feel convinced that there is something in it. The drenching business, too, is a dirty one when a very weak dog is the patient, and what runs out of his mouth and dries upon him seems to nauseate him too, beyond all remedy. Stimulants, I have long since discontinued. Spirit, if retained, has at the best a very temporary effect, and when that effect has worn off it leaves the patient in a worse state than before.

The great secret is to offer the right kind of food and, by means of coaxing and encouraging, get him to eat a little. I have found that there is always something which will be eaten voluntarily, but the great difficulty is discovering what that something is. There is usually thirst with distemper, so that if bread and milk, or rather milk and bread, be kept about he will take a lap occasionally if for nothing else than to slake his thirst; if he does he is getting some little nourishment at the same time. Chicken and rabbit broth are excellent, and a little of the flesh is frequently much appreciated. Sometimes, however, these varieties of flesh will be stubbornly refused, but fish will be snapped up with avidity. Beef and mutton should not be offered. Both these will cause the temperature to fly up. Eggs are inclined to cause biliousness, especially when beaten up. On no account in distemper, or for some considerable time afterwards, should anything hard, such as biscuits, be given.

The third week is the convalescent period, and here again great care must be observed, for with returning strength often comes sharp hunger and a desire for a big meal. Little and often is the motto now, and when you have discovered what the patient wants most, feed him with it every hour if necessary and he will be round the corner in a few days and ready to jump over the house. So much so, in fact, that the inexperienced invariably allow him to do so and wonder why he should have died after making so excellent a recovery. After a week of convalescence no dog of mine would ever smell the open air for at least six weeks to come. If your dog after distemper be permitted to take his freedom under six weeks, results are bound to be fatal. If death does not take place at once the dog is left with some sequela of distemper which necessitates his being killed.

From a too early dismissal from hospital ensue fits, chorea or palsy. Even an apparently small measure of exertion seems to upset the brain and nervous system in anything under six weeks from convalescence.

During the whole course of the disease it is most important to wash out the mouth twice daily and thoroughly cleanse the teeth. If the teeth are not attended to they become covered with a brownish coating, which must be of some very acid nature as it completely destroys the enamel, leaving the teeth permanently discoloured and shelly. The eyes, too, should have very special attention for the discharge, if not removed frequently, will destroy the eye and even cause entire blindness.

In certain forms of distemper the feet become affected insomuch that they are soft and putty-like to the touch and ooze a thin and colourless serum. The skin or horny covering of the pads later on becomes as hard as iron and feels very much like the shiny leather with which chairs are covered. When this happens, the pads eventually crack all around the edges and the entire surface peels off. This is a most favourable sign. With proper precaution after convalescence, I have never known a dog to die who thus shed the skin off his feet.

Another favourable symptom is a breaking out on the inside of the thighs, which should be encouraged rather than otherwise. The eruption should be sponged daily, morning and evening, with nothing but clean warm water. The idea should be to remove the dried discharge on the broken pustules in order that they may continue to discharge. It is unwise to use disinfectant as it may have the effect of healing the places, and, instead of allowing the poison to come away from the system, may drive it back.

The whole discharge in distemper is an effort on the part of Nature to get rid of the poison which is either the cause of the disease or bred by the disease. The eye and the nose are the chief vehicles for carrying away the poison in the form of discharge, but where the skin is thinnest it will also make its appearance, if the eye and nose are not capable of dealing with it all.

When a breaking out takes place on breast and chest it is not a favourable symptom. I think it means that when eye, nose and thighs cannot of themselves get rid of the poison and the thicker skin is called into use, there is so much poison that the case is hopeless. It is invariably the rule, unfortunately, that when the thicker skin breaks out the patient does not recover.

It is a moot point if in distemper the patient should be given access to water. Personally, I am of the school which withholds water, but at the risk of perhaps giving wrong advice unintentionally I feel that I must give one instance of my experience.

It was in the plague ridden October of 1918 when man and dog went down in their thousands. The saplings died off in spite of every care, and day by day the kennels became more destitute of dogs. The thing became a nightmare and it became fairly obvious that there would be few survivors. I was willing in the end to let the sick dogs do what they wanted, and one very hot middle day two seven months' saplings in more or less the last stages of the disease staggered out into the yard and went straight to the water trough. It was in the sun and the water had certainly the chill off it. One dog began to drink, and I have never before or since seen a dog drink to such excess. He drank until he looked like a balloon. To stop him, I had not got the heart. I felt he was bound to die like the others had done and I felt that he might die as happy as possible if water gave him pleasure. Presently, when I did not think it was physically possible for him to drink another drop, he stopped and, turning away, looked stupidly and vacantly round. Fearing the end I went towards him and found that he was preparing in the orthodox grey-hound fashion to be properly sick. I had no time to get out of the way of the stream of water which might from its force have come from the blow-hole of a whale. I should say that every drop he drank he forced from his inside with incredible force and with it a quantity of slime almost unbelievable. Meantime, his brother had been proceeding to empty the trough, and before I could again get clear I got the shower bath from the other. Unnecessary to relate, I never wore that suit again. Both dogs recovered from that moment, and were well on their legs within a week. The day following I let a bitch, almost at death's door, go to the yard. She also drank until I thought she would burst, and she recovered also. It is painful to me to this day to think of the beautiful dogs I lost and the expense to which I went to save them when they all might have lived had they only been turned out to water. There seems little doubt that the water acted as an internal bath, and removed the slime which was slowly choking and clogging the inside. Perhaps, when all is said and done, the dog knows best what to do, and many deaths may be caused by our anxious desire to do for him what we think he cannot do for himself. With reference to the taking of food when he is in the mood and my practice never to drench, I think this was suggested to my mind after the water episode.

Distemper is like a cold in ourselves, although the cold is not attended with the same fatal consequences which we have to make up our minds may be met with in distemper in the dogs. It is, however, in common with

a cold, a catarrhal affection which has three stages. A
cold lasts nine days, distemper twenty-one. With
reference to the cold it is " Three to come and three to
stay and another three to go away." Substitute seven
for three and you have distemper in its three stages
also. With reference to "the cold" so-called, if
you can detect its coming on immediately by the peculiar
tickling in nose and throat you can cut it in the bud by
filling a jug with boiling water and putting in some
disinfectant such as lysol, then placing the nose over the
steaming jug with a bath towel over the head and in-
haling the steam. If, however, you try this plan say in
an hour, the chances are that the cold has proceeded
on the first stage and entrenched itself so strongly that
nothing on earth will make any difference to it. It
must then run its course. In distemper we have the
same idea. If it is possible to spot it immediately
upon its entry into the system and can employ the salt
and water, or even the soda, all may be over at once,
but if a few hours on the way it then resolves itself
into a case of nursing and fighting the disease, and if the
dog is not willing to respond you might as well give up
the effort. The two ways in which the dog can best
assist is by keeping up his spirits and eating a little from
time to time. This I think he will do if not forced at
the wrong times and by being kept as cheerful as possible and made to forget his troubles.

## CHAPTER XVIII

### WORMS

As it is not the purpose of this book to be in any way a veterinary work, I am not taking the diseases and placing them in order as I would otherwise do, in groups with reference to the various parts of the anatomy and the various systems, but am taking only the outstanding well-known diseases with which all are familiar, and which cause the greatest havoc in our kennels.

Worms would, I think, if put to the vote, probably be made to rank next to distemper from a point of view of mischief wrought in our kennels. Personally, I am strongly of opinion that more dogs succumb from worms and the effects of worms than from distemper. When distemper comes, either because it is of a particularly virulent form or from neglect or inexperience in its treatment, dogs die off in great numbers, making distemper appear to be the most deadly of diseases, but if it were possible to keep a tally of the whelps which die at anything from a day or two old up to three or four months, and the older stock which die from fits, malnutrition, chronic skin trouble and disorders often mistaken for distemper, all of which can be traced to the presence of worms, it is fairly certain that the number of deaths from worms would exceed the death roll from distemper.

It is most important, therefore, that every owner should give the maximum of attention, not so much to eradicating worms but to taking steps in the prevention of worms. That " prevention is better than cure " is one of the sagest proverbs ever invented, provided that we have sufficient knowledge of the difficulty in question as to its origin and sources so that we can be armed and well prepared against its attacks. The worm is a most elusive gentleman (or lady as the case may be) and be as careful as one may, it is well-nigh impossible to bar it from its natural habitat, the intestine of the dog.

Speaking generally, there are three species of worm common to the dog, namely, the tape worm (two varieties), the round worm and the maw worm. There is a third variety of tape, but it is very rare, and in addition to this we have another rare worm, known as the kidney worm.

Each worm requires its own particular treatment, for what expels one has little or no effect on another. There is no vermifuge on the market as a proprietary pill or ball or capsule which will act on tape, round and maw worm with equally good results. There are some excellent worm pills which act like magic on round worms, but as all the pills known to me contain the drug combined with the purge, none of them is useful in the expulsion of the tape worm.

Worms may be present in the dog for a long period without any being passed, but there are symptoms exhibited by the dog which tell us plainly that they are there. A general raggedness in appearance, and a dry staring coat with a deficiency of flesh in proportion to the food consumed, are the invariable signs of worms. The constant passing of small quantities of fæces by the dog when at exercise is another indication, as are small hard lumps of fæces covered with a gummy, frothy coating. The droppings should be examined carefully for traces of worms, and the owner or kennelman should ascertain definitely what species of worm it is which he therein finds. If it is a tape of either variety the treatment will be the same.

The dog should be taken in hand at once. Each night or morning for at least three days he should be dosed with Epsom salts. The tape worm creates in the intestine a jelly-like substance in which he embeds himself, and while thus ensconced the worm is proof against his enemy, the oil of the male fern, which is the deadliest poison to the tape. Now if Epsom salts be given as suggested it causes a flow from the bowel which clears away the jelly, leaving the tape worm open to attack.

The dog should be fasted for twenty-four hours before the giving of the medicine. This is absolutely essential if a complete cure is to be effected.

The only satisfactory drug for tape worm is the oil of the male fern, which should be given in capsule form. If given in emulsion, being most nauseating, the dog invariably vomits the dose and thereby gets no benefit from it. There are splendid capsules on the market prepared specially for human use which can be procured from most chemists, and these cannot be bettered. Twelve drops of the oil should be sufficient for an adult greyhound. The box usually has the capacity of each capsule on the cover. If it does not state the number of drops contained it will always be well to enquire from the chemist to how many drops of the contents the capsule is equivalent.

The action of the male fern is as follows:

The coating of the capsule having become dissolved, the oil is released and in due course it finds its way into the intestine and begins slowly to poison the tape worm. The tape is firmly secured to the walls of the intestine by means of the suckers from his head, through which he derives nourishment for himself by sapping the system of the dog. It will take at least six hours for the male fern to do its work, but by the end of that time the worm should be dead. But not until the worm is dead do the suckers relax their grip upon the wall of the intestine. When, however, they do release their hold the tape worm is a dead mass only waiting to be slid out. This can best be done by warm castor oil. Provided that the preparation with the salts has been thorough, that the twenty-four hours' fast has been rigidly observed and the oil of male fern has not been stale, a dose of warm oil six hours after the capsule should produce a perfectly complete tape in its entirety. A careful examination should be made for the head. The head will be found to be of about the size of a small horse bean. The whole worm should be consigned to the fire, for it contains sufficient eggs to infest the whole of the country. Although the worm has been poisoned it is not at all certain that the fertility of the eggs has been impaired.

If the head is not removed this extraordinary parasite, in nowise dismayed, proceeds to grow for itself a new body of equal or greater length than that of which he has just been deprived.

It is with reference to the removal of the head that the average proprietary pill is so utterly useless. Whether or not it contains male fern or one of the other drugs which act on tape worm, its action is wrong. The usual manufactured pill contains the drug and the purge combined and acts in anything up to twenty minutes. As it has been proved that the tape worm has to be subjected to the poisoning effect of male fern for at least six hours, it will be appreciated that little or no good can be done by a pill or otherwise which acts in twenty minutes.

Most of these pills produce a splendid evacuation of worms and the average owner, being impressed with the quantity, quite overlooks the fact that the chief trouble may not be present in the clearance. The chances are, too, that if the head is expelled by means of a violent purge without the worm first having been destroyed, the dog may suffer from trouble in the intestine through the suckers having been torn out rather than having let go after life was extinct in the worm.

The round worm is next in importance in order of seriousness in effect upon the dog, but nowhere approaching the tape worm as an element of evil. However, even the round worm should have no house-room in the dog, and as soon as his presence be detected, out with him bag and baggage.

In appearance he is not dissimilar to the ordinary garden worm, and varies in length from an inch to six or seven inches. He is not a lonely object like the tape, who lives by himself in solitary state, but is usually found in fairly large numbers, as a rule in a ball, one mixed up with the other in a perfect tangle. The round worm is prolific, depositing an enormous number of eggs with which to stock countless other hosts in weeks or months to come.

The round worm is not attached to the intestine with suckers as in the case of the tape and is, in consequence removed with much less difficulty, but not with ease. The same careful preparation is necessary as that in the case of the tape. The salts should be given for the three days prior to the vermifuge, in the same way, and

M

the twenty-four hours fast should be observed, but the medicine in the case of the round worm should be santonine and powdered erecanut instead of the male fern.

The dose for an adult greyhound should be two grains of the santonine and ten to twelve grains of erecanut. The mistake is made universally of giving the santonine and erecanut mixed, whereas the santonine should be given first and after an interval of two hours the erecanut should then be administered. In a further interval of two hours it is well to give the dose of warm oil.

The best mode of administering santonine is to place it in a bolus of treacle rolled in flour and slip it down the throat. The erecanut can be disposed of in the same way.

Erecanut is one of the safest and most efficacious forms of vermifuge, and it is at the same time the least expensive. A pound of the nuts can be purchased for a few pence and, provided that they are kept dry, will keep for years. If you have a large kennel where worming may have to be done at frequent intervals it is a good plan to carry a nut in the pocket, and when required all that has to be done is to grate some off on an ordinary nutmeg grater.

So far, we have considered the matter of the expulsion of worms, but if it were possible to protect the dog against the invasion of those pests, a much more useful object would be achieved. Beyond, however, a brief outline of the natural history of the various worms, it is impossible to go, and we can only make use of the knowledge which we have of their mode of life in taking the necessary steps to guard the dog, as far as we can, from getting into the danger zones where worms are active and ready to take possession of his interior.

Before proceeding to describe the strange and complex life of the worm, I am bound to mention one medicinal remedy at least. I am not prepared to say that it is a certain preventative, but I am greatly inclined to the opinion that it is. My information on the subject was gleaned from a Belgian who came as a refugee to this country in 1914, and in his own country had been a successful trainer of police dogs. He for a time took over the management of my own dogs here. He was strong on the subject of worms, and held the theory that if the dog were thoroughly cleansed of worms and then given a section of garlic every day, there would be no possibility of re-infection.

Most people are familiar with garlic and know that the bulb is made up of many small sections. These sections break out easily and are of a fairly uniform size. One of these only is to be allowed per dog. It should be grated over the feed. The dog seems to enjoy it rather than otherwise. While this man had charge of my kennels I must say that the dogs looked well at all times, and I cannot remember any time in my experience of dogs when the expenses account was lower. I conclude that worms, being absent, the food went further and did more good, and as other items for drugs had not to be considered, I am of opinion that many of the minor disorders for which we have to be purchasing medicine at all times are due in the main to the presence of worms.

It will be remembered that shortly after the war there was a great case brought by a leading daily paper against a firm dealing in a patent medicine, the healing properties of which were said to be due to the essential oil of garlic contained therein. It was decided in court that there was really nothing connected with garlic in the preparation. We are not at all interested in a controversy now so old, but the interesting matter of moment to our own present subject is the fact that garlic came into the picture so much at that time goes considerably to strengthen the theory that it may be a safe preventative against worms. At any rate, garlic has fine tonic properties and a small section daily, if it does not stop absolutely the encroachment of worms, will be useful as a health-giving adjunct to the evening feed.

Generally speaking, there are two varieties of tape worm common to the dog—as I have already stated, the *tænia serrata* and the *tænia cucumerina*, and the natural history of each is practically the same. In order that the owner may guard as far as possible against his dogs coming too closely in contact with the sources from which they may pick up the worms, I will outline very briefly what happens in the development of these pests.

The *tænia serrata* consists of a head and a body made up of separate segments or joints, each being of a squarish shape. When fully developed the *tænia serrata* can shed separately any of these segments which passes out through the rectum of the dog. By its own muscular motion it can detach itself from the fæces in which it left the intestine of the dog and creep away by itself to any reasonable distance, usually to the nearest grass, where it gets dried up, releasing its millions of eggs to stick to the grass upon which some of them, or perhaps the whole segment, will be swallowed by the rabbit, the hare, sheep, cow or other herbivorous animal. In the stomach of any of those animals the eggs quickly hatch, and, by means of their boring propensities, soon reach the blood vessels of the animal and are presently transferred to their natural seat, where they are found in the form of cysts, whether it be in the intestine of the rabbit and hare, the brain of the sheep or calf, or the liver and lungs of ruminants, or the muscular substance of the pig. These cysts, as found in the intestines of the rabbit and hare, and the embryo found in the brain of sheep and cattle, and the muscular substance of the pig, quickly becomes developed worms when at last transferred to their natural habitat, the intestine of the dog.

Let us consider therefore the various sources from which the dog may contract tape worm. From the point of view of greyhounds, the most likely source would appear to be the rabbit and hare, for when a kill is registered the average keen dog will tear his game open and eat if given half a chance.

As pollution from this source cannot be guarded against, what cannot be cured must be endured. We can, however, guard against the cysts and embryo being swallowed while active, by cooking all flesh and never giving it raw. The stock of worms is largely maintained by the offal eaten by dogs which hang around slaughter-houses and the dumps where butcher's offal is deposited. Then, again, a productive source of transfer of cysts or embryo is the vessel in which the raw flesh has been placed in the cookhouse. Sheep heads, let us suppose, are brought in and placed in a basin. They are left there over night perhaps, and after having been cooked they again find their way back into the same basin which has not been scalded out meantime. Here we have a very likely means of conveying into the dog that which will, in a short space of time, be a fully developed tape worm.

The *tænia serrata* in the dog is identical with the form of tape worm found in the human (*tænia solium*). Tape worm in the human in our country is very uncommon as compared with the number of people affected on the Continent, and the reason probably is that we do not eat semi-raw ham, etc., in the same way as the inhabitants of the Continent love to do. The tape worm so prevalent in Belgium, France and Germany is no doubt largely derived from the pig.

The round worms so commonly infest the dog as to make their presence the rule rather than the exception Unlike the tape worm, which is male and female in one and fertilises its own eggs, there is, in the round worm, male and female, the former being much smaller than the latter and requiring contact with it to fertilise. As I have already said, the round worm closely resembles in appearance the garden worm. It is pointed at each end but the ends are slightly flattened. The natural history of the round worm is peculiar. As soon as the eggs are matured they are passed into the intestine of the dog, and thence into the world in the fæces, and remain in a torpid state in some heap or cess pit for months if necessary, until they find their way to stagnant water, where the complete worm soon makes its appearance in the shell. The formed worm does not, however, burst the shell as in most other forms of life, but abides its time until swallowed by the dog in water, when it eventually reaches its natural habitat the intestine. It has been proved that the worm in the shell can support vitality for as long a period as a year, and that in varying temperatures.

The most fertile source, therefore, from which a dog can contract round worm, is water. It is unwise, for other reasons, to allow the greyhound to drink while at exercise, but if for no other reason than the prevention of round worm he should never be allowed to drink from ponds, or in fact any water while out, and in kennels all the water should be boiled. So strong are the provisions of Nature in preserving life that the round worm is as surely protected as any other form and is bound to find his home at last, but, we can, nevertheless, take precautions against the achievement of his purpose in so far as in us lies.

The maw worm, which is not supposed to be the cause of any serious trouble in the dog, has at times been considered by naturalists to be shed segments of the tape worm of one or other variety, but this is not very likely to be correct. The shape does not indicate that it has any connection with the tape worm.

However, the remedy for maw worm will be the same as in the case of the round worm, and as there is no theory that the maw worm, if not harmful, is in any way beneficial, the safest course is to clear it out.

Baffling as are many subjects connected with worms, the most puzzling of all is how the worm can be present in the newly-born whelp. That it does exist in whelps at birth is beyond dispute, but how they get there is a mystery as yet unexplained. The final stage of development of the worm takes place in the dog. The eggs are thence passed out and have to pass through another host before again being transferred to the dog to complete development, and this being a recognised fact, nobody can say how the unborn whelp can become infested. The presence of the round worm is even more difficult to explain than that of the tape worm, for in the case of the latter we have seen that the eggs, after they have been hatched by virtue of their boring propensities, find the blood vessels and by their agency get transferred to their proper seat. It is possible that these might find the circulatory system of the bitch and find their way into the whelp, but they, after all, have to reach its intestines. In the case of the round worm, however, we have seen that this worm makes its entry into the dog in the shell. We must just accept, therefore, that worms do exist in the newly-born whelp, and the only practical course to follow is to watch the growing youngster and take steps against the worms when it becomes apparent that they are present. If worming can be deferred until the whelp is eight weeks old, so much the better, but it happens frequently that the matter requires attention long ere that.

# CHAPTER XIX

## SKIN TROUBLE

FROM the point of view of the mischief caused, skin trouble will come next on the list of obstacles which come in the way of the average owner.

I use the term skin trouble advisedly.

Skin trouble may be divided simply into two classes, viz., contagious and non-contagious. The contagious form is mange, which, happily as regards numbers of cases, is well in the minority. The non-contagious form falls into the category of follicular mange, and for the want of a better term eczema, of which there are various varieties, all known by specific names to the dog owners, such as blotch, surfeit, red mange, etc., etc.

With the exception, however, of follicular mange. which is a disease unto itself, all forms of non-contagious affections are better to be known as skin trouble until it is decided by the microscope if contagious or non-contagious, for without its aid it is extremely difficult in many cases to discern mange from one or the other forms of what we call eczema.

Mange (*Sarcoptes Canis*), called sarcoptic mange, is a contagious form of skin trouble and the one most dreaded by owners. Undesirable as is the outbreak of mange in a kennel, there is this consolation about it, that if properly tackled the cure is more easily effected than is the case with reference to the more obstinate forms of non-contagious skin trouble. Mange, being contagious, must not be trifled with, for it quickly spreads from one dog to another. The mange insect gets into woodwork, and although it is now fairly well established that the insect does not live there for any appreciable period, the fact remains that it does manage to support vitality for a time, and it may be that the eggs remain ready to be hatched for a much greater period.

The mange insect makes for itself a burrow or gallery in the skin of the dog, and at the end of this gallery, by means of the microscope, the male and female can be seen sitting together. The eggs of the insect are very large and adhere to the legs of the female until they are deposited in the burrow by her. The eggs quickly hatch, and each insect makes a separate gallery for itself, making the life of the dog a misery to behold. The itchiness of the skin gives him no rest by night or by day, causing him to be scratching and biting at himself continually. Sarcoptic mange is of a scabby appearance, which increases rapidly, and if not attended to soon covers the whole body, by which time the dog has become emaciated through loss of blood and the entire absence of rest.

The most efficacious treatment for sarcoptic mange is a dressing made up as follows: eight ounces of petroleum jelly, eight ounces of cocoanut oil, four ounces of boracic acid powder, four ounces of flowers of sulphur and six teaspoonsful of oil of tar. The petroleum jelly and cocoanut oil should be mixed by applying heat. When they have been reduced to a liquid state by stirring, the oil of tar should be poured in and stirred through. The vessel in which the melting has been done can then be removed from the fire, and the boracic and sulphur having been mixed, stirred into the liquid. This dressing should then be left to thoroughly cool, when it will set into a fairly firm paste.

Every scab on the dog should then be dressed with the ointment. A mere smearing on of the dressing is not sufficient. It is a tedious and unpleasant task dressing a case of mange, but unless done properly it might as well be left undone. The scab, it must be remembered, although produced by the discharge consequent on the activities of the insects in rendering their house into what we know as a festering sore, is a provision of nature in protecting the inmates, for the excretion, when it hardens into the scab, is proof against most dressings unless applied vigorously. The plan to adopt is to take some of the dressing on the tips of the fingers and firmly but gently apply friction to the scab, rubbing it until it comes off. This will be found to happen easily in the end and to cause no bleeding.

The softening property of the oils, aided by the harder material of the sulphur, softens the edges of the

scab and gradually detaches it from the skin of the dog.
The antiseptic is then enabled to reach the seat of the
trouble, the insect being conveyed thither by means of
the cocoanut oil, which is the vehicle. The gallery is
literally flooded with death-dealing materials which
quickly put an end to the life of the parasites. If the
dressing is properly done, all the parasites should be
destroyed on the same occasion. It is expedient, however,
to give the dog a thorough washing in warm water after
three days, and it is not a bad plan, to make sure, to
dress him once more. A week at most should be sufficient time to effect a complete cure, and as petroleum
jelly and cocoanut oil, in conjunction with some form of
carbolic, constitute the finest hair restorers in the
world, a new coat should in the same time be well on
the way.

The universal idea that mange is difficult to cure
comes largely from the fact that useless dressings are used
as a rule. People, especially those who keep dogs in
their houses, have a strong objection to the greasy
forms of dressing because of the mess which is occasioned
by the animal which has been treated, and, in consequence, there has always been a great inducement for
manufacturers to produce dressings neither oily or
greasy; but, so far, to my knowledge, no satisfactory non-
greasy dressing has as yet been put on the market.
Sulphur, too, appears to be indispensable to any
dressing which is efficacious.

Mange having been diagnosed, the dog should be removed from his kennel and treated in some other, and in the meantime the affected kennel should be thoroughly disinfected by being scoured down with carbolic acid. Every nook and crevice should be thoroughly attended to and the kennel left empty for a few days, for carbolic acid, or in fact any form of carbolic, crude or otherwise, has strange and often fatal effects on dogs. Dogs are most susceptible to carbolic.

I had on one occasion to cleanse a kennel with carbolic acid. The disinfecting was done in the afternoon and after which the door was closed. Two days later the dogs were returned to their kennel and on the following day were showing symptoms of carbolic poisoning. The kennel had dried out perfectly and sawdust had been put down, but the air was still heavy with the fumes, no doubt coming from the woodwork, and by breathing the carbolic-laden air mild poisoning resulted. It is a fact, lso, that too much carbolic added to the bath will poison a dog by absorption through the skin. This is doubly likely to occur in cases of skin trouble where the skin is in an unsound condition.

A dog which has fallen a victim to mange should, in addition to being dressed, have his food increased in quality and quantity. The mange parasite takes heavy toll of the dog's blood, making it necessary to build up the patient for some little time afterward.

FOLLICULAR MANGE, although non-contagious, is

parasitic also, but the insects are not the cause of the disease but merely consequent upon it. Follicular mange is hereditary. It is without doubt the most obstinate and certainly the most loathsome of all the forms of skin trouble with which we are acquainted.

It is so obstinate in its cure that it is almost universally held to be incurable. A dog once certified to be suffering from follicular mange is usually on the advice of the vet. put down immediately. Follicular mange is not, however, incurable. It takes a long time to effect the cure, but it can be done. The pity, however, is that as the disease is hereditary, no matter how good your dog or bitch may be, and no matter how anxious you may be to breed therefrom, the chances are that you will be breeding animals almost sure to exhibit the hereditary disease at some time in their lives.

Follicular mange begins by the discharge of a nasty smelling serum. The skin becomes wrinkled and thickened and horrible pits and sores make their appearance in the creases. These sores give off a smell which makes the weak of stomach sick. The sores continually pour forth evil-looking pus, and dust and litter and everything which will adhere sticks upon it. A more loathsome sight than a dog in follicular mange is difficult to imagine. The discharge clings to the hair, gathering it into bunches which feel like a brush on which gum has been allowed to dry. If one of those bunches be taken between the finger and thumb and pulled, it will come away, having rotted absolutely from the roots. I have seen dogs with discharging sores from the skull to their uttermost extremities covered absolutely with open sores, and others with dried pus and the legs so wrinkled as to bear no resemblance to the legs of a dog whatsoever. These were cases where the owner had a mistaken idea of love for his dogs. He had not the heart to destroy them, but did them a much greater injustice by allowing them to live under such disgusting conditions of life.

Follicular mange is not at all common, for which we should be truly thankful, but I understand that in the slum districts of London and the other large cities, the various societies working for the welfare of animals see a good deal of the trouble and put down a great number of dogs every month. Under more healthy conditions very few cases appear, but we can conclude that many a dog predisposed to follicular mange escapes it simply by virtue of his more fortunate conditions of life. The dogs who are ill-tended and who live perpetually in dingy streets and alleys, being predisposed by nature to follicular mange, contract it in greater proportion.

The treatment of follicular mange, so far as a dressing goes, will be the same as in the case of sarcoptic mange, but it is not to be thought that the cure will be effected in a week or a month.

One dressing will destroy the parasites, which, as we have seen, are only hangers-on in the camp of the

"Platinum" ("Beaded Dick"—"Tip Top Lass"), 1927 W.bd.b. This bitch holds the record at Clapton for 700 yards, winning in 45.20 secs. by 7 lengths. The property of Mr. J. H. Martin.

"Greek Proverb" ("Latto"—".Sarre Beechie"), 1926 F.d. Since leaving the coursing field this handsome dog has had two races on the track, winning each time. The property of Mr. J. H. Martin.

*Photo by]* [*Thos. Fall.*

" Teterror " (" Heavy Blankets"—" Concerto II "), 1926 F.d., shcrtly being retired to the Stud, has won six races, one match and cup against the Midland crack " Kinsman." The property of Messrs. Edney and Winslade.

*Photo by]* [*Thos. Fall.*

" Barna Skipper " ("Cheerful Speed "—"Fluff and Puff)," 1926 W.f.d., winner of three races out of four on the flat. In trials over hurdles he has shown great merit. The property of the West Ham Racecourse Ltd.

germ of follicular mange. The slaughter of the parasites causes a change in the process of the disease and this is usually looked upon as a symptom that a cure has begun. This, however, is wrong reasoning. The disease may be still as active as ever, and all that has happened is that the irritation of the parasites having been removed there is less discharge and what remains is not similar. This is as to the matter produced by the disease and the parasite together.

Now, in the treatment of follicular mange, it is not only the sores and pustules on the exterior which have to be attended to, for a drug administered internally is of equal importance in the cure. Nobody knows what the actual cause of follicular mange is, but we do know that arsenic is necessary, and a long course of that drug is essential to a cure. The difficulty, however, about giving arsenic at a time when a sulphur dressing is being applied should not be lost sight of. Arsenic and sulphur combined is a deadly poison to the dog. It is a case, therefore, of doing one thing at a time or leaving the arsenic alone in favour of a usefully strong tonic and an increased diet of nourishing food. Milk is one of the greatest helps in curing this obstinate disease. I know of one case which was cured permanently, simply by means of the dressing and a diet consisting of flesh and milk. Sometimes the flesh was cooked, but usually it was given raw and the patient had at all times a quart of milk in front of him.

N

The fact is established beyond any doubt that follicular mange is non-contagious. An affected animal may sleep with others free from the disease without the slightest possibility of their contracting it. Attempts have been made scientifically to infect one dog from another by means of transferring the serum. This, in the case of sarcoptic mange, can be performed without difficulty.

THE NON-CONTAGIOUS forms of skin trouble are altogether more difficult than mange. In mange you have an insect which you jump upon and kill out of hand, and the trouble, except for healing up the entrances to the galleries, is at an end. In other forms of skin trouble, as we are never very sure of the cause, it is much more difficult to prescribe a cure.

One thing there is which stares us in the face in non-contagious skin trouble, and that is, that there is something in the system of which it wants to get rid, and proceeds so to do through the medium of the skin. We know that skin trouble can be promoted by an insufficiency of nourishment. We know that, on the other hand, it can be produced by an excess of food and too little exercise. We also know from long experience that too much exposure to the sun is another productive source of a particular form of skin affection.

Since the vitamin was captured there have been many experiments carried out regarding affections of the skin. One commercial firm engaged in producing baby food has discovered from experiments on rats, that a rat fed on a diet free of vitamin develops skin trouble which in all its stages resembles very closely what happens in the dog suffering from what is called eczema. The absence of violet rays has also been found at the same establishment to be the cause of skin trouble. Skin trouble, apart from sarcoptic and follicular mange, I am of the opinion, is due to a lack of nourishment, light and exercise rather than to overfeeding.

The two generally accepted forms of non-contagious skin trouble are known specifically by the names of " Blotch " and " Surfeit."

BLOTCH, which is due to too much condition with insufficient exercise, usually makes its appearance in the greyhound after he has come out of strong work for a rest and his food both as regards quantity and quality has not been changed to meet the altered conditions.

Blotch is known by the thickish serum which appears amongst the hair and the scab which ensues.

Blotch should not be dressed. What the system is endeavouring to throw off should be allowed to come away freely. If blotch is dressed it amounts to driving back what is trying to come out. Instead of dressing treat the dog internally by administering a cooling purge and change the quality of the food to something more in keeping with his requirements when he is doing little work.

SURFEIT is probably due to improper food entirely. This disease is frequently confounded with mange because it resembles mange in appearance. If taken in time the duration of the trouble need not extend beyond ten days. The treatment is first of all to change the diet and give an ounce dose of salts twice a week.

As I have already said, both in the case of blotch and surfeit, it is an attempt on the part of nature to get rid of some poison in the system. While a dog is yet perfectly clean from skin trouble, it is possible in various ways to say definitely that an attack of skin trouble may be expected at no very distant date. Usually, nature fixes upon the part of the skin where it is thinnest in order with the greater facility to discharge the serum. The flank is a particularly favourite spot for pustules to make their first appearance. Let us take the skin of the flank where it is to be found in a double flap alongside the belly, between the finger and thumb. If the dog is healthy and not making up for skin trouble, the two skins where they overlap will rub smoothly one against the other with an even, oily feel. Let the dog be making up for an attack of blotch or surfeit, the feel will be vastly different. When the two skins are rubbed together the feeling will be that there is something of a cordy nature between them. This feel, which comes with experience, is an absolutely certain sign that skin trouble will appear ere long. There are other tests, too, such as certain glands which will be found to be greatly enlarged both before the attack and while it continues. There are several other ailments of the dog which are closely akin to skin trouble. A discharging eye, ear or nose may be the safety valve which just saves a breaking out of the skin. Frequently in the non-contagious forms of skin trouble there may be a badly discharging eye, ear or nose simultaneous with the breaking out, and if this be the case, the chances are that the trouble is likely to be of shorter duration. Sometimes, on the other hand, when nature decides that all the serum be discharged through the ear, it will take considerable time before the ear is again clear. I have on several occasions observed that dogs were due for an attack and have noted that a discharging ear has come before the breaking out of the skin. Having watched carefully the progress of the trouble, I have noted that when the ear ceased discharging the normal feel of the flank and size of the glands have returned. This makes it fairly obvious that the serum, which would otherwise result in skin trouble, can be discharged through the ear or eye. This discharge from the ear is not to be confused with other affections of the ear which have nothing to do with skin trouble, but usually to the invasion of the ear by tiny mites, which create a jelly substance in the root with a smell like bad cheese and also looks cheesey.

The discharge which is allied with skin trouble comes in great quantities and is found in hardened masses in the ear, completely covering the flap in the morning. I have even known the flap of the ear to become full of pus itself and seem like a filled bladder. This kind of discharge should not be stopped, but, on the contrary, should be encouraged. The best treatment is simply washing out with clean warm water and a little spirit of wine. It is important to keep the affected parts clean, but it is not wise to introduce disinfectants in case the aperture from which the discharge is coming should be healed up.

When the eye becomes the vehicle through which the discharge is made to leave the system, great care has to be taken two or three times daily to keep that organ clean and free from matter collecting on it. If the matter is permitted to remain in the eye from day to day the chances are that the sight will become affected, and blindness is usually the result of inattention in this direction.

Although the non-contagious forms of skin trouble are easily cured (comparatively speaking) if taken in time, they are most obstinate when they become chronic. The fact is that if the trouble goes on for some length of time dirt gets into the broken pustules and sets up a new trouble of its own in which germs, having nothing to do with the disease, take possession and set up a kind of blood poisoning. This, when it occurs, has of course to be dressed, and the dressing already referred to will be found to meet the case admirably.

Cod liver oil is a factor to which the trouble yields with great success.

The eruption between the toes which often attacks greyhounds is only another form of the same trouble. Here again we have thin skin, and the serum selects the spot for getting out. The best treatment for this eruption is bathing in warm water, simply for the purpose of keeping the feet clean and removing the serum which is discharged. Nature should at the same time be helped in her efforts by a good dose of salts given twice a week.

A greyhound is frequently seen with a tail bleeding at the tip. Great ignorance prevails as to this. The average kennel man will tell you that the dog had knocked his tail. So he did, but why? He knocked it by shaking himself so violently that his tail came in violent contact with the walls of his kennel. Why did he shake himself so vigorously? Because he is going to have skin-trouble. A dog with the tip of his tail showering blood all over everybody who comes within three or four yards, may look in condition but he will not look in condition long. Try the flank of that dog and you will find the feel which I have just been speaking of.

The bleeding tail is to the skilled a warning message that the dog should be taken in hand at once, and if this be done the attack of skin trouble can be avoided success-fully.

The entire tail at times becomes full of the serum, which will frequently become concentrated at a point about the centre of it, forming a swelling as big as a pigeon's egg. Rot will here set in, and it is not un-common for the tail to break and have to be amputated from the point of affection down. At other times the tail will swell throughout the greater part of its length to nearly the thickness of the tail of a calf and become rotten throughout. Although the skin of the tail would appear to be thin it is evidently more proof against the serum getting through than is the skin on any other part of the body. Provided that it can get an outlet at the tip the swellings just referred to are avoided. Skin trouble recurs, and in the case of a dog who has had half his tail removed, when the next attack comes' if it settles into the part of the tail retained, great swelling is the invariable rule, owing, I think, to the skin growing strongly over the blunt extremity left from the amputa-tion and making the tail more or less a secure bottle for the serum. This serum, wherever it comes, is greatly inclined to occasion rot of the part where it is discharged.

Every intelligent owner has observed at times a speck of hard excretion on the points of the ears. Ter-rier and gun-dog men will always tell you that this is due to the ears having been torn by thorns through the dog hunting in cover. Nothing of the kind. The excretion is dried serum which is finding its way out slowly through the thin skin at the tip of the ears. This discharging of matter goes on for lengthy periods, gradually increasing, until morning by morning quite a wad of dried matter can be removed, sometimes leaving the skin red and sore. Everyone has noticed dogs with a V taken out of the edge of the ear. That V is the point where the serum used to be discharged which gradually rotted away the skin and flesh, leaving the V shaped niche.

The ear of the greyhound, which should be as soft as silk, fine throughout and with pleasantly soft edges, is, when the dog is not in perfect health, furred round the edges; that is to say, there is a thickening of the edges which, when felt, feels rough, while a finger rubbed on the inner side of the edge removes a greasy substance. This again is the dried serum, which is slowly being exuded. The dog may look perfectly well in every other respect, but it will invariably be the case that he will not be just as he should be in his coat. It probably lies nicely and may be soft to the touch as it ought to be, but when rubbed with the hands a grease will be found adhering to the palms in miniature wormlike rolls. Exudation of serum to this extent may make no material difference to the dog, but, nevertheless, I would vote him just the slightest trifle under what could be his best form. By many this grease from the coat is looked upon as dirt and a bath is resorted to, but all the baths in the world will not clean away the grease, for as you remove one lot more is actually in process of coming forth. It is to the inside you must look and not the out.

When a case of skin trouble does not respond to treatment, it is probably due to the presence of worms. Worms in the dog are as likely a cause of Surfeit as improper food.

A greyhound which has been lying lazily around for weeks if suddenly given a long gallop will invariably break out in skin trouble.

Skin trouble in the young whelps of six or eight weeks old is not uncommon. When this occurs, a carbolic dressing must not on any account be used. It is almost bound to end fatally. There is a very simple and absolute remedy. Take half a pound of best fresh butter and mix it with a liberal allowance of boracic acid powder and thoroughly dress the whelps, taking care to remove all scabs merely by the action of rubbing in the butter. In two days the whelps will be clean and entirely free from disease. This remedy, known only to the favoured few, is safe and sure. The whelps may lick it, but if they do it only seems to act as a first class internal lubricant and antiseptic.

## CHAPTER XX

### COMMON KENNEL AILMENTS AND ACCIDENTS

THE more intricate ailments, difficult to diagnose, I am not going into in detail because it is better in the case of a dog looking out-of-sorts to call your professional man at once. If you can tell him fairly accurately when the trouble started and how, as it is his job to diagnose and treat, he will do both much better than you can.

There are a number of ailments which, once seen, or even described, can never be forgotten. They are fairly common and it is well that each should be given a few lines here.

CHOREA, a common sequel to distemper, is likely to make its appearance at any time. This disease is easy of diagnosis. It takes the form of a twitch which usually settles into one of the legs. When a leg is affected, the twitch is continuous when the dog is at rest but may be almost unnoticeable when he walks, trots or gallops. From time to time rumours are heard of remedies which are said to be the certain cure for chorea, but up to the present I have no proof of a complete cure. Occasionally chorea becomes less acute and one or the other of the remedies gets the credit, but the real reason for the improved condition is due entirely to the improvement in the strength of the dog, his general toning up in condition as regards his general health and in his nervous system, the low state of which was the primary cause of the chorea. There is, however, no complete cure for chorea which has been at all severe.

In addition to chorea coming on as a sequel to distemper, it can be set up in the puppy by worms. I have seen several cases of twitch in puppies which, after the removal of worms, has disappeared almost as suddenly as it made itself evident.

This twitch I do not believe to be chorea proper. The irritation of the worms, I think, sets up pressure on a nerve causing a twitch, and when the cause is removed the twitch goes also. Chorea is not confined to a leg, but may settle into a jaw or eye. When it is a leg, the dog when standing will raise the affected leg from the ground and move his paw up and down as if beating time. This applies more particularly to a forefoot. When a hind leg is affected the dog will frequently keep this on the ground, but the twitch can be plainly seen and very distinctly felt in the thigh muscles.

Chorea in the mouth can be pardonably overlooked. The mouth can be comfortably shut and the chorea can be detected in many cases only by taking the muzzle in the hand, when the regular twitch will be readily felt.

When the twitch is in the eyes, this is easily seen and equally easily felt. The twitch is not actually in the eye but in the eye-lids and just over the eyes, sometimes appearing to cause the whole skin on the skull to move.

A greyhound affected by chorea is not worth keeping. It is a nervous disease and connected with the brain, the centre of the nervous system. As we have already decided, no matter what the strength and perfect shape of the dog may be, if he is wrong nervously, he is wrong altogether. A greyhound which has chorea in a jaw, it may be argued, is sound as regards his legs and feet, heart and lungs and in all other respects, but this is not so. There is always a lack of self-control where chorea exists. It may be that the dog is addicted to sudden and nervous bouts of barking. It may be that he is unable to lick out his feed bowl or that he has lost control over his inside, being neither able to hold his water or his other motion. In fact a dog suffering from chorea is independable in every way.

Bitches with chorea should never be bred from. Happily, most of them are non-breeders.

COUGHS, altogether apart from that in distemper, are not uncommon in the kennel, and although attended with little or no danger to the dog are very often the cause of his doing badly in courses and races in which he ought to have done well. The cough is usually a symptom of worms. If a dog is looking tolerably well and not off his feed when the cough is heard, prepare him for a vermifuge, and the chances are that after the removal of the worms there will be no more coughing.

The cough is often heard when the dog is on the lead and not at any other time, except perhaps for a half hour or so after the collar has been taken off. It is often erroneously supposed that it is the action of the collar when the dog pulls that causes the cough, and those under that misapprehension allow the cough to continue for months and it only gets removed when the dog comes to be wormed. The pressing of the collar certainly does provoke the coughing, but it is not the cause.

Cough mixtures are a waste of money. If the cough is due to worms all the cough mixture in the world would not cure it. If the cause is worms, then the cough disappears automatically when the cause has been removed. There can be few animals which suffer more acutely from catarrh than does the dog, and it is certain that there is no other upon whom the effects of catarrh is a greater hardship. It must have been obvious to every intelligent and observant dog keeper that a dog has not the power to spit. I have watched dogs on very many occasions labouring under severe bouts of coughing and have pitied their abortive efforts to rid themselves of the phlegm. In bad cases, when a paroxysm of coughing comes on, nothing is more distressing than to see the dog trying his utmost to cough up the catarrh which is slowly poisoning him. He gets it up so far and just at the juncture when one wants to say " Spit it out," the effort ceases and the injurious bacteria-filled filth goes back into the stomach. Vomiting is a perfectly natural act on the part of the dog, and fortunate it is, for only by means of that act is it possible for him to avoid the slime of which he may be full. This peculiar slime, with which the dog seems at all times to be infested, has not as yet occupied the attention of the scientists who investigate canine diseases, but it is bound in time to be considered by the more thinking and observant men of the profession. It is that self-same slime which is the crowning disaster in distemper. If taken in time, as we have seen in the chapter on distemper, it can be cut with a dose of common table salt in water. In the case of the cough, apart from distemper, an emetic works wonders, but great care must be taken in administering an emetic when a dog is suffering from a cough. If an attempt is made to pour anything down the throat when coughing is actually taking place it is very possibly the case that the drench will enter the wind-pipe, causing instant death by suffocation. In the absence of worms (if that can be wholly possible) a cough can be incurred by the dog being allowed fast exercise suddenly after a spell of idleness. After such a happening, when the dog pulls up you can actually hear the slime gurgling as his wind comes and goes, just as though there was a bubble interfering with his breathing. There is nothing attended with more danger to the dog than sudden exercise after weeks or months of idleness, and one of the chief troubles which ensue takes us on to a further kennel ailment which there is no trouble in diagnosing.

FITS are frequently the sequel to distemper owing to the invalid being allowed out too soon. Fits thus coming on close the scene. There is no further hope of recovery.

Worms are not infrequently responsible for fits. Remove the worms and there may never be a return of the trouble, but once a dog has had a fit I am greatly afraid that, at some distant date perhaps, there may be another.

No greyhound, whether a racer or a courser, is ever likely to get into the same state as the companion dog which has spent eleven months in the town without ever having been out for a trot until removed to the country with the family for the summer holiday, but it does not take eleven months to accomplish what happens to the family dog. On the first day of the holiday the poor dog is allowed to gallop *ad lib.*, his master looking on and deceiving himself into the belief that Binks is having the time of his life. He is, no doubt, and in all probability his life may be rapidly nearing its end, for such violent and prolonged exercise after doing nothing is almost certain to produce a fit.

The dog drops suddenly and lies struggling on the ground, frothing at the mouth. He will get on his legs after a short space, stare stupidly round and perhaps yelp somewhat, and quickly regain consciousness, going along as though nothing had happened.

Special care has to be taken of all greyhounds which have been out of work, and particularly of brood bitches and dogs which have been at the stud. Too little attention is bestowed upon the bitches. They are allowed to slop around and are taken little or no notice of until they next come in season and are allowed to get into a sluggish and unhealthy state. On going to a new home they are frequently fortunate in having that amount of attention given to them which is lavished on a new toy, and they often pay the penalty by having a fit or fits after a gallop which they never ought to have had. If you are going to do your bitch well and keep her happy and fit by the proper amount of judicious exercise, do not take the fresh acquisition out until you have cleaned her out thoroughly and tried her for worms, and even after that bring her to it gradually by giving her so much road work on the lead and never allowing her to distress herself when loose in the fields. If she appears to be doing too much call her up and put her on the lead for a space and then give her a little more freedom. In cases of fits I am a believer in the use of aspirin.

JAUNDICE is a trouble in which I have no great personal experience, having had only two cases : one of

o

those was a terrier and the other a whippet, but the strange coincidence is that I had both cases at the same time although in different parts of the establishment, which was a large one. I have never had a case in a greyhound, but have seen plenty in other kennels which appear to get jaundice as regularly as they do distemper—probably their jaundice is almost entirely in conjunction with distemper.

It is, I am inclined to think, a fairly hopeless and disheartening disease to treat, as it invariably ends fatally. We must never anticipate trouble too much so we must cure jaundice when it comes or, at least, do everything in our power to that end.

The stages of jaundice are as follows: Great dullness in the animal and white or clay-coloured evacuations will be the first symptoms. These mean that the liver is not acting. If taken at this point the jaundice may be cut through a dose of any saline. Glauber salts, which act directly upon the liver, is probably as satisfactory as most other things. It is, however; speaking generally, not until the yellow tinge of the eyes, lips and pads makes its appearance that anything out of the way has been observed. By this time the dog has become yellow in his skin, the liver has become properly congested and the secretion of bile arrested. The only hope now is to stimulate the liver to its proper functions, and in this there comes the difficulty, in the greyhound particularly, for, owing to his formation, his liver being well covered by his ribs, it is difficult to get at for the pounding and kneading processes that cannot be surpassed in this obstinate disease. Some authorities believe in an emetic upon the ground that the mechanical action of the dog when he heaves brings an action to bear upon the liver, but this action or necessary friction is so brief that I do not attribute much significance to it. When jaundice takes possession the dog goes off his feed rapidly and loses strength at an alarming rate, which makes the attempted cure doubly hard. If the liver can be got at, the most satisfactory treatment of all is to work it with the hands, squeezing it and squashing it unmercifully, always with the one intention of softening it and removing the congestion.

It will be necessary each night and morning to give a dose of saline. The compound rhubarb pill is still held by many to be a specific. It will be difficult to get the patient to feed, but as he will be thirsty it is usually possible to get some nourishment into his stomach by means of white of egg and water given in small quantities from time to time.

With reference to the two cases I have had in my own kennels, I saved the terrier (sealyham), but lost the whippet. The sealyham I saved purely, I am sure, because I was able to get at his liver. It was enormously swollen and enlarged, and protruded beyond the ribs, making it possible to seize it in the hands. He also appeared to appreciate being drenched with Glauber salts, took his white of egg and water willingly and made an excellent recovery, notwithstanding the fact that the weather was wet and that, owing to a drain being blocked, the end stall of the stable where he was isolated, flooded, and I found him enjoying life up to his belly in the water. This, according to all theory on the subject, should have ended his life, but it did not. The whippet was most disappointing. He was one of those beautifully made dogs, well ribbed up and with great depth of brisket. The liver, protected as it was with the fine chest, was impossible to handle. The salts were returned almost immediately upon being put down, as was his food. The end was not long delayed.

There is a famous authority on greyhounds who has judged all the big meetings and bred the best dogs in the world, whose experience it has been to have a wave of jaundice every year and to lose much young stock annually. He informs me that jaundice is contagious and infectious and that it is carried by rats.

RICKETS, as will be seen hereafter, constitute the bugbear of the kennel: once recognised, a recurrence in subsequent seasons should be guarded against.

# CHAPTER XXI

## RICKETS

THE disease of the bone known as rickets is one which, if not guarded against, is likely to prove the undoing of the coursing enthusiast and the racing man as well, for young stock which has had rickets is never any use for either game.

Rickets is due in the main to improper feeding or to dark and unhealthy housing and confinement generally. Even when the most ideal food is given if the whelps are brought up in the dark rickets is found to ensue. This is more certain to be the case than in that of the imperfectly fed whelps reared in bright healthy surroundings.

Prevention being better than cure, the obvious course to adopt is to rear the whelps properly. If rickets should appear, the cure is not easy and usually leaves the greyhound considerably under first class form.

In the adult greyhound, badly sprung ribs, and legs not quite straight, are indications that the whelp may have been rickety.

The symptoms of rickets are enlarged joints and poorness of bone. Large knotty joints in the whelp are a sign of good bone rather than otherwise, but the main shaft of the bone must be strong and stout in keeping with the joints. If the joints are large and knobbly, with the ends of the bones very round and the shaft above thin in proportion or bowing outwards or inwards, then you know that the whelp has rickets.

The theory to-day is, so far as food is concerned, that the whelp is not getting the necessary vitamin to assimilate the lime which is essential for bone making.

Codliver oil or the manufactured extract of codliver oil which contains the necessary vitamin, now so largely used for racehorses, is said to be the best remedy in cases of rickets, and many successful cures are reported.

It is when the whelp has attained sapling age, say eight or nine months, that the enlarged joints are to be taken as serious symptoms of the disease, for after this age it is most difficult for the animal to make sufficient bone. Even if he fines down, he is left with bone of poor quality which is very liable to fractures when the dog is put to great strain, either in jumping or stopping himself at his turns.

The toes, too, which should be strong and stout, are thin in comparison with what they should be and are inclined, whenever the dog is at all low in condition, to go flat and splayed.

A dog which has suffered from rickets is seldom if ever of any use, so that it is futile to deal with the subject and recommend any particular treatment beyond what I have already said. To get healthy, robust stock, do the brood bitch well and judiciously, for the development of the whelp before birth is as important as its life after birth. Codliver oil is good, but it can be overdone to the point of nauseating the bitch, but the vitamin concentrate is tasteless and can be given with confidence. If it is a preventative against rickets, for what it costs, it can be money well spent to include it in the ration of the bitch. If the whelps are fed rationally, as arranged for in an earlier chapter, and managed as they should be, there can be no danger of rickets setting in, but the whelps should be guarded against any possibility of the disease with as much care as the average owner would reasonably take against their getting distemper when that scourge might be avoided.

The accidents which may befall a greyhound may be summed up in cuts, tears, bites, fractures and dislocations. All of these are only too common.

As regards injuries to the skin and flesh, I am now entirely convinced that the best method is to leave things to nature.

Wounds from cuts, etc., heal in a marvellous, not to say miraculous manner if left to themselves. A cut, bite or tear, no matter how bad it may seem, I now leave and never stitch. Keep it clean as far as possible; the light and the dog's own good judgment, coupled with his proclivity for healing up unaided, will do the rest.

Much is now known regarding the value of the

violet rays, but the dog, if left to himself, in time of stress knows more about the subject than do our leading scientists. I guarantee that a dog which has sustained some grievous cut or tear will avoid sleeping in a dark corner if he has but half a chance to settle down elsewhere. If I had a greyhound which, let us say for the sake of argument, staked himself in such a way that he was showing his entrails, and even if it were possible to stitch it, I would leave that dog alone. I would allow him to find his own position and that position I would be willing to wager would be in the lightest part of the building. Given a comfortable bed that dog would lie there and would probably refuse food for days, but at the end of that time he would get up whole.

In severe accidents in the region of the abdomen, dogs will invariably adopt the line just referred to as did primitive man and as does uncivilised man to-day. Provided they are healthy, in the light and without food, so as to avoid the necessary getting up to evacuate, the injury will heal.

In coursing, the greyhound is subject to cuts on the legs, and oftentimes such cuts, although not serious, are a heavy handicap to him in running or following courses. Collodion is one of the best remedies. Half an hour or so before running apply collodion to the cut freely with a brush, bringing the edges of the wound together and keeping the leg still for several moments afterwards in order to allow the collodion to set. The application will usually suffice to carry the dog through his course.

Friar's balsam is another application which is useful, but not so good as the collodion.

Unless you have had some experience in the use of splints or plaster, it will be best at all times to find the nearest vet. for a fracture or break.

Dislocations are, in a way, easier, but some little practice is essential even to replace a joint. A dislocation of the hip is at all times a difficult job and one which tries even the skill of the professional man. It is indeed often necessary to put a greyhound under an anæsthetic in order to replace a dislocation of the hip. If the operation is left for two or three days it is pretty well impossible to replace the joint as it will in that time have formed a new socket. The dislocation of the knee or stifle is not quite so difficult but even here, unless you are good at it, it is much better to send for a vet. or take the dog to him and have the thing done properly.

In these days of rapid conveyance and with a vet. never more than a few miles off, it is futile to attempt to instruct novices by means of writing how to set a limb or replace a dislocation. The only thing which is useful is to instruct people as to the nature of the various injuries: I visited a kennel once where a dog had lain for two days with a broken hind leg and the lady who owned him did not know that it was a break. There cannot be many people who cannot recognise a break, but in case there are some, let me say that if the injured limb be shaken it will swing from the part where it is broken. A dislocation is, if anything, more difficult to detect, but usually the head of the joint can be felt distinctly as being out of socket.

## CHAPTER XXII

### WEIGHTS OF GROWING GREYHOUNDS

WHELPS having come through the troubles of weaning successfully should weigh at ten weeks old from eighteen to twenty pounds, dogs, the bitches just a little less.

From this age onward the experienced breeder will be able to tell from day to day and week to week if his youngsters are making satisfactory progress, and that merely by looking at them. Many of the men of this calling may have no knowledge whatsoever of what the approximate weight at varying ages should be, but they know exactly if that weight is less than it ought to be. *Experentia docet*, of course, but for the benefit of those who are rearing their first litter, or it may be their second or third unsuccessful attempts, I propose to append a table of weights as they occur as between three months and ten months. These figures have been collected from various quarters, and as they coincide almost exactly with my own personal experience in weighing whelps they may be taken as correct.

If the weights which I shall lay down are found to be exceeded at any stage of growth that will be all to the good, but if they fall short by any appreciable amount at any time, it will be a bad sign, for in the majority of cases, if say, the weight falls short by three or four pounds, the chances are that it cannot be made up by maturity.

Distemper, if this scourge should intervene, will make a material difference to the smooth and regular progress of growth, and all that one can do is one's best; but it is an up-hill job when the growth of a greyhound is retarded. If much weight is lost at any one time, I am not going so far as to advise the novice to get rid of his whelps (although I am almost tempted to do so), for there have been some notable instances where greyhounds, thrown sadly back, have developed into very beautiful and successful animals.

The 1925 litter by " Skeats " out of " Onward Anzac " is a case in point. This litter had distemper very badly, and for some weeks looked so backward that its members were counted out as likely to be of no use. In March of 1926, however, Mr. Joseph Walker advised me as a friend to buy a brace of the litter, stating it as being his honest opinion that they would be runners. He said they were still under-sized and stunted but that he had observed a distinct movement in growth and thought that with the warmer weather at hand they might jump into growth. His opinion was correct. One was " Golden Sultan;" The other, " Golden Spark," having been purchased during the summer by Mr. Gordon Smith.

The novice must therefore use his own discretion as

to what he does, but he will find that greyhounds which make up lost time will be in the minority.

The best method of weighing whelps at three months, and probably at four months also, is to put them in a canvas bag and hang it to a set of steel-yards by a string. Once in the bag the whelp will keep still—but accidents may happen in getting him into the bag.

From five months, the most simple and at the same time the most satisfactory method of weighing is in a sling.

The necessary sling any saddler will make, but without ever going to the trouble of having a sling specially made, the weighing can be accomplished equally as well as follows:

Procure two canvas horse girths, of which let one be six inches shorter than the other. Pass the short girth round the loin and the other round the chest between the fore-legs to keep it from slipping backwards. If you will then bring all buckles together by means of a piece of cord, the dog can be suspended from the hook thereby. The best plan will be found to stand the dog on a box or table placed under the hook and then when the cord has been placed upon the hook, gently remove the box or table, which will leave the animal suspended in mid-air. He will not struggle.

The weight at ten months will be, within a pound or two, the dog's running weight. The weights as given hereafter will obtain when the whelps are in best condition. The presence of fat will make some little difference.

Between the dates of weighing the owner must be guided by his eye and hand as to the condition of the whelps. If a check is suspected steps must be taken at once to remedy the evil, whatever it may be, for the next date of weighing cannot be awaited. If a whelp is off his feed the necessary dose of oil must be administered immediately, because one feed missed means loss of weight, no matter how minute.

If whelps are feeding but losing tone, a tonic must be resorted to forthwith. I am greatly opposed to a tonic in the nature of drug pure and simple for growing stock, and would always advise one or other of the preparations which come under the heading of patent foods such as Virol. A week of this treatment, which will cost at the outside a few shillings, may save several hundred pounds. However, if whelps are fed in the rational way and managed as I have directed, there ought to be little recourse to expensive preparations in the maintenance of their well being. We must, however, bend to the scientific knowledge which has undoubtedly produced many forms of food so prepared that it is easily assimilated, and may just be the very thing required at a critical juncture in the life of the whelp.

Common-sense goes a long way, and the average young owner, whose heart is in his hobby, should not go far wrong when he knows what the desired rate of progress should be from month to month. The greater trouble is, however, that so many beginners fail to notice instantly a falling off in condition. As I have already said, there are many old hands who, although they are the finest judges in the world of condition and development, could not tell you to within pounds what weight a whelp should be at any particular stage of his growth. Yet let one of those see a litter which is not his own, one which he has never seen before, and he will tell you straight off the reel if they are well or badly grown. " How old are they ? " he will say, and when you mention the age he will say : " Not big enough for the age," and what he says is almost invariably found to be correct.

Table of weights of dogs and bitches between the ages of three months and ten months :

| DOGS. | | | BITCHES. | | |
|---|---|---|---|---|---|
| At Three Months | .. | 23 lbs. | At Three Months | .. | 22 lbs. |
| ,, Four | ,, | .. 32 ,, | ,, Four | ,, | .. 28 ,, |
| ,, Five | ,, | .. 40 ,, | ,, Five | ,, | .. 34 ,, |
| ,, Six | ,, | .. 50 ,, | ,, Six | ,, | .. 41 ,, |
| ,, Seven | ,, | .. 53 ,, | ,, Seven | ,, | .. 44 ,, |
| ,, Eight | ,, | .. 58 ,, | ,, Eight | ,, | .. 48 ,, |
| ,, Nine | ,, | .. 62 ,, | ,, Nine | ,, | .. 51 ,, |
| ,, Ten | ,, | .. 64 ,, | ,, Ten | ,, | .. 54 ,, |

It will be observed from the table above that the ages of from three to four months and again from five to six months are the times of most rapid development.

The more gradual advance between four and five months is a provision of nature to afford some little rest after the demand which has been made upon the system generally in the growth of the previous month. Between the ages of four months and five months, and again after six months, nature can be assisted in her work by the owner giving slightly increased attention to the whelps in the way of special nourishment and food easily digestible.

Any discrepancy which may be found with regard to the table will be with reference to bitches rather than to dogs, for at the present time there is a tendency to find bitches going over the orthodox weight.

"Chain Mail" (" Guard's Brigade "—"Cutty Mark "), 1925 R.f.d., holds the record at Harringay for 500 yards flat. He is an honest consistent performer on the track, with a good deal to his credit in the coursing field. The property of Dr. McFarlane.

" Wykon" ("Mardale—"Woodsia "), 1925 Bd.d., a good winner on both the Show Bench and the Race Track. The property of Mrs. N. C. Runge.

"Tinas Boy" ("Let 'im Away"—"Playful Gipsy"), 1923 Bd.d., a prominent Clapton hurdler; also winner of a coursing stake at Kempton (Devon). The property of Mrs. E. Laer and Mrs. E. Garland Wells.

" Satanic " (" Sans Souci "—" Lady Irene "), R.f.d., a popular Clapton Stadium favourite, and winner of several matches. The property of Miss D. Garland Wells.

## CHAPTER XXIII

### MEASUREMENT OF POINTS

SCHOLARS in anatomy are concerned more with the measurement of the points of a greyhound than is the coursing or racing enthusiast, but it is necessary that the subject should be touched upon here. Weight, however, is the important factor, and if this be correct we can be satisfied with our dog if his symmetry is right, or, rather, if we have an eye for symmetry. The measuring of a dog is a tricky task to undertake. I am certain that it is only one man in ten who can measure a greyhound correctly, even if he knows a greyhound and has experience in the use of a tape or rule. With a perfect rule and spirit level, I have known three men to measure the height of the same dog and each make him a different height. When it comes to measuring a neck, for instance, greater mistakes can be made and so on over all the different points.

A different return of the height may be due to how the dog may be standing, and a wrong measurement of neck will probably be due to the fact that no two men will take it accurately from the same point. We have heard more about measurements since racing came, for it was thought that one way of keeping a record

P

of a particular dog as a protection against substitution was to make a chart of his measurements. This plan was worse than useless. In addition to inaccurate measurements having been taken at one track, the dog would change in condition probably before going on to another, and over a great number of cases where measurement was relied upon it might have been a different dog, so utterly different were the measurements in question.

I propose to give a few of the important and minor measurements, but not with any idea of misleading the novice that if his dog does not answer to them there may be anything wrong.

Taking the ideal size of a coursing dog to be sixty-four pounds, his height will be approximately twenty-six inches from the ground in a straight line to the point of the shoulder. Condition makes a great difference. A dog which in tip-top condition stands twenty-six, when badly down may quite possibly measure half an inch to an inch less than that figure.

Measured after a severe course the same remark will apply. Exhaustion or low condition spell the same result. Dealers in polo ponies know all about what exhaustion will do to get an over-sized pony measured in at fourteen two.

The back of the greyhound, being one of his chief points for usefulness, we take next. From the shoulder point to the buttock will be twenty-eight to thirty inches, made up of fifteen inches from shoulder point to last rib and from last rib to buttock thirteen to fifteen inches.

The girth of the chest, another valuable acquisition to the greyhound in which to keep safe his heart, lungs, liver, etc., is the same measurement as the length of the back, tweny-eight to thirty inches. Fitness or lack of condition here again plays a great part. Fatness completely alters both.

The length of neck is from nine to ten inches, but to measure the neck of a greyhound is about as difficult as trying to make an accurate measurement of a live eel.

Length of arm nine inches (same as neck). From the knee to the ground four and a half inches.

Girth of loin eighteen to twenty inches in running condition.

From upper thigh to the ground is roughly the same as the height and made up approximately thus : Upper thigh, ten-and-a-half inches; lower thigh, eleven inches; hock to the ground five to six inches.

The circumference of head between eyes and ears will be around fifteen inches, but if the dog be measured again, say, when in the last stages of distemper, a great surprise will be experienced. If for identification purposes a dying dog was measured at this point what the tape would show would not be that it was the dog measured originally and which showed fifteen inches girth around the head.

These measurements are useful only in this way :

that an owner should possess some general knowledge as to his hobby. Just in the same way it is interesting for him to know that the dog has forty-two teeth, made up as follows :

On the top jaw twelve molars, two canine and six incisors; on the bottom jaw fourteen molars, two canine and six incisors.

Although it is more in the province of the veterinary man to know thoroughly of what the skeleton consists, it is yet nevertheless interesting for the owner to be able to say that the skeleton is made up of skull, trunk, and extremities. The skull is hollowed out to contain brain, eye, ear, nose and tongue. It is attached to the trunk by the neck. The neck is the beginning of a canal extending from the head to the tail, made up of hollow bones which contain a continuation of the brain known as the spinal cord. This canal, known as the spinal column, is divided into the seven cervical, thirteen dorsal and seven lumbar vertebræ and extending backwards still further into the sacrum or rump bone, attached to which is the tail, made up of its own twenty bones, which are not hollow nor have anything to do with the spinal cord. To the thirteen dorsal vertebræ are attached the thirteen ribs which, together with the breast bone, form the thorax or chest. By the same kind of ligamentous attachment, as that by which the ribs are fastened to the vertebræ, the hip bones are made secure to the sacrum for the protection of the bladder, and the uterus in the bitch, and to give a firm fulcrum to the hind legs for the purpose of propulsion.

There is no collar bone in the dog. The only attachment between the fore legs and the body is muscular, so that the chest is, as it were, slung between the shoulders on the fore legs.

The fore leg is divided into the shoulder blade, the arm, the forearm, to which the foot is attached by means of the pastern, answering to the palm of the hand in man. The knee corresponds to his wrist.

The hind leg is divided into the stifle or true thigh, the leg or lower thigh and the hind pastern terminating in the foot.

## CHAPTER XXIV

### EXPENSES OF REARING AND TRAINING

THE young coursing or racing enthusiast will probably want to know what his outlay is likely to be before he can bring a dog of his own breeding into the field or on to the track.

The only difference in expenditure between producing animals for coursing and those for racing will be in the price of the brood bitches and possibly the stud fee.

A brood bitch of the right blood, if we are going to breed coursing greyhounds will cost at least £100. Many have been sold for £200 and up to £400 in recent years, and one famous bitch was reputed to have been sold last year for £800, but this was by private bargain and the price cannot be vouched for. She had previously produced a Waterloo Cup winner, but she herself was originally purchased for the modest sum of £5.

It is, however, the expert alone who can risk buying a cheap bitch and by his superior knowledge mate her to the right dog and produce fliers.

The brood bitch for producing racing stock will cost less than one for the other purpose. Let us, however, base our calculations on what will be expended in breeding coursers.

Let us assume that the term of usefulness of the brood bitch will be four years. Assuming that she cost £100, £25, quarter her price, will be the first item of expense. The next will be her keep for one year, say at 6s. a week, £15 12s. Next there is the stud fee, which may be anything from £7 7s. to £26 5s. If we strike an average of £14 14s., including travelling expenses, we have the next outlay complete. Then, assuming that the litter is one of six, and that they are whelped in January and go out to walk at the beginning of March at 6s. each for fifty-two weeks, our next item will assume the magnitude of £93 12s. The next step, the saplings being now fourteen months old, is to place them with a trainer for the summer at 10s. per dog for five months, £60, and after that, assuming that a brace is ready to go into strict training, for two months at 12s. 6d. each, we have a further £10 on their account, and the 10s. each running on for the four others, £16, we arrive at the grand total of £234 18s., or an average of just around thirty-seven guineas per dog by the time the first runner enters the field.

At the present price of greyhounds this average would just represent a selling price which would yield a return of the outlay.

It would be an exceptional litter which would give the breeder six winners, but four out of the six can be reckoned upon to pick up stakes, and as they are presumably well bred there should be at least one first-rater

amongst them, in which case there should be a sub-
tantial profit on the venture.

I have based my calculations upon the whelps being
put out to walk, as this is the cheapest and best course. If
one is fortunate enough in putting whelps out at 6s. each
per week, that is infinitely less expensive than rearing at
home, unless the owner can give all his time to their
management. If, however, he is a business man, he
will of necessity have to employ a man or boy to look
after the litter, and at the present cost of labour the
minimum for wages which he must face will be not less
that £1 10s. per week, and it is certain that he cannot
feed the whelps for the 6s. difference between that sum
and the 36s. per week paid at walk. He is certain, too, of
running much greater risk from epidemic if he keeps
all six whelps together at home, so that, taking everything together, the walk system is the cheapest and
best.

On the other hand, if the owner be a farmer or engaged in some other work where there is spare food for
the dogs and free run, the account will of course be
less than that calculated above, but at the outside, if the
whelps are properly done, I cannot reduce the expenses
by more than £25, for greyhounds cannot be reared
successfully on refuse, and even if they are fed at the
wholesale price of commodities, that costs money. If
it is consumed it is not sold.

He who sets out to breed racing dogs will get let down

just a shade more lightly than he who ordains to breed coursers, for the former will not have to face the same outlay for a brood bitch. £50 should suffice to acquire a bitch, and the maximum stud fee will not exceed ten guineas.

The charges for walking will be the same, but further expenses will cease when the saplings have come in from walk with, of course, the exception of the £1 per week training fees on the track, which includes entry fees as well, and as dogs are eligible to race at fourteen months the racing man escapes the 10s. per week per dog for the long five months of idleness between March and the time when the coursing dogs go into actual work preparatory to the beginning of the season. The expenditure, therefore, for the purely racing owner amount to £12 10s., quarter price of the bitch, her keep for a year £15 12s., stud fee and travelling say £6 6s., keep of the six whelps for fifty-two weeks £93 12s.; total £128 until the time when the first dog is ready to race. It will be seen, therefore, that breeding for the track is very considerably cheaper than breeding for coursing—but it cuts both ways.

The coursing man stands the chance of having a first-rater in his litter which may become a more than ordinarily profitable animal; he has three others which are passably useful, and probably after picking up several minor stakes will sell for a great deal more than the average thirty-seven guineas they cost to produce, and even if the two remaining are hopeless as coursing dogs, they may be in truth racers of the highest order. The dog bred for coursing purposes has the two fields open to him according to his temperament; he is either a good or bad courser, and, if the latter, can go to the track. The dog which is scientifically bred for the track, as far as we can see at the present stage of racing, has no other vocation open to him but racing. We know that the bad coursing dog often makes a successful racer, but it remains yet for it to be proved that a bad racer will make a good courser. The thing may happen, we do know; but the majority of the English dogs which have gone from the coursing field to the track are animals which would not have been bred from had there been no racing.

He who is content to breed one good litter a year is more likely, I think, to be successful than he who sets out to breed many litters with the object of winning many laurels instead of the modest few.

The moderate purse can run to one first class bitch and to send her to the best dog; but when many are desired it takes a long purse to acquire the best, so that in its absence the tendency is to purchase less classical animals, relying on what is known as " A Hit." That is to say getting a good one chance bred. It does not pay. The number of failures which ensue wipe out any profit or glory there may be in regard to the few successes. Whether it be for field or track, my strong advice is to limit your liabilities. Breed only from the best, do them well and look for the just reward which will not fail. After all, even if you are a millionaire, it is not a sportsmanlike procedure to endeavour to collar every big stake during the season to the entire exclusion of those not so well provided with this world's goods as you are yourself. The motto should be " Do a little but do that little well."

# CHAPTER XXV

## THE SHOW GREYHOUND

No work on the greyhound would be complete without some mention of the family which has come to be known as " The Show Dog."

The home of this family is Cornwall, of which county the greyhound has been a native since ancient times. The greyhound may be said to be the national dog of the Duchy. An old charter under which certains lands there are held, directs that a brace of greyhounds has to be delivered to the Duke of Cornwall as part of the terms of the tenure. This custom is carried out to this day, and the form is gone through with all due solemnity, but the greyhounds are always returned by the Duke at the close of the ceremony.

The Cornish dog differs in many respects from the legitimate greyhounds of the country. I mean by " the legitimate " dogs, those which are registered in the greyhound stud book. Few, if any, of the Cornish family appear in that volume. There is no coursing under National Coursing Club rules in Cornwall. There is coursing of a kind, but that is carried on privately and approaches the standard of rabbit coursing more nearly than anything else. That is to say, the kill is the determining factor in the course. It can but be so, for, although the Cornish dog is capable of a fair turn of speed, he is sadly deficient in working qualities and staying ability. However, it would not be fair to criticise them too severely, for they have ceased to be working dogs and are merely exhibition animals and very delightful companions. In the eyes of a not inconsiderable school of admirers, they are held to be of great grace and beauty, but to the coursing man, who looks more for utility qualities than accentuated good looks, they are not held to possess what he must regard as outward charm of appearance.

One of the chief attributes in a show dog is great size. Breeding for this has been carried to a pitch bordering almost on the ridiculous. If we take the ideal size of a coursing dog to be sixty-four pounds weight and around twenty-six inches at the shoulder, it will readily be realised what the difference in size between that and the show dog is when it is stated that the latter will scale seventy-four to seventy-six pounds and go up to between twenty-nine and thirty inches at the shoulder. A dog of this size has to be an exceptionally good one to attain any great success in coursing. Few there are which have ever done anything of note. " Harmonican " was over seventy pounds, and was, up until 1927, the best Waterloo Cup winner of modern times. He was an exceptional, big dog.

The abnormal size of the Cornish dog is interesting
and worthy of some attention in passing.

The origin of the gigantic specimens which are to
be seen at all the premier shows came about thus. As
we have seen, greyhounds have been the proud possession
of the Cornishman since early times, and until some
forty years ago were more or less like other greyhounds.
If anything, indeed, they were smaller and finer than the
members of the other families in England and Scotland,
but at about that time there was a vicar of St. Columb
Minor, near Newquay, Cornwall, who had a fine kennel
of Scotch deerhounds. The Cornishman, loving a
lurcher equally with a greyhound, and always being ready
to avail himself of an illicit service, lost no opportunity
at St. Columb Minor, and made a point of conveying
his bitches thither to get an infusion of the blood of those
handsome dogs of the north which in so many respects
resembled the greyhound and even excelled him in outward beauty of outline. The crossing which there took
place is therefore the landmark to which we can look back
for the forebears of the show dog of to-day.

As a sporting dog, the show greyhound has all but
ceased to exist. It is not only that his conformation
militates against his chances of success in the chase,
but his very inclinations to pursue and kill are sadly
lacking through disuse.

Let us consider for a moment the ways in which his
conformation and bulk handicap him in his work.

Great height being essential, a dog with too much daylight under him has been produced, and a dog of this description is unable to turn at all easily. When he has to come round sharply he either requires a forty-acre field in which to do it, or he rolls upon his back in a smaller space.

Another essential which is demanded in a show dog is an exaggeratedly deep brisket. In an earlier chapter we have shown that brisket of abnormal depth will bump upon the ground in uneven places when the dog is fully extended, and this is so much the case in the Cornish dogs that I have seen a dog cut himself to the bone in an endeavour to overtake a rabbit.

The gun-barrel front and tightly-fitting elbows, so much in vogue in show dogs, are other factors which hamper the dog in his movements for, although we all like a good fronted one, there are limits.

The strangest freak in the make-up of the Cornish dog is his disinclination to follow the lawful calling of every good greyhound. His lack of fire may be due to two causes, the first being the excessive amount of inbreeding which has been done—and probably even then to animals of poor fire—and the second is that the dog, ever since he became a show dog, has been purposely kept from his game.

A fetish of the show ring is that dogs must be shown with lean shoulders, and this they cannot have if allowed to gallop, as they become muscled up on the shoulder.

In consequence the Cornish dog seldom or never gets a gallop. He therefore seldom sees a hare. If he is a good specimen and looks like making up into a champion, he is taken in hand at a tender age, four months perhaps, and led daily at a slow pace preparatory to being got ready for puppy classes when he is over six months old.

Last year, when there was a great demand for unregistered dogs to go abroad for greyhound racing, Cornwall was denuded of most of her greyhounds, and it is a fact that more than fifty per cent. of them had to be returned as they would not chase the electric hare. It was argued by some that those dogs were so superlatively clever that they recognised the absurdity of an attempt to catch the mechanical hare, but this hardly holds water. From amongst the registered dogs which came green to the tracks there were very few which did not chase the hare. The Cornish dog is essentially a show dog and as such we must treat him. He has never had a great measure of popularity as a breed, but he has had a staunch following at most times, and when judging is in progress at the big shows the greyhound ring is always one which is well lined with spectators. If the greyhound has never been in the forefront as a popular dog he has never been entirely in the doldrums, as is the case in so many other breeds which attain to world-wide popularity for a short time and then go out entirely.

Wonderful prices have ruled for many years for really good specimens such as " St. Blaise," a famous Champion of a few years ago. Miss Dorothy Beadon gave ninety guineas for " St. Blaise " when unshown and Gertrude, The Lady Decies, gave high prices for " Larchmond King," whom she made a Champion, and for " Scotswood Sylph," an enormous bitch. Americans have always been carried away by our show greyhounds, and practically every good specimen which has come into prominence in our shows has gone across the Atlantic at very remunerative prices. Prices upon the whole were good even for mediocre specimens of the class for shows under championship class. So far as the requisites for a show dog are concerned, there were very few really bad specimens in Cornwall.

Q

## CHAPTER XXVI

### HOW TO BREED AND REAR A CHAMPION

THE breeding of a champion for the show ring is not attended with so many difficulties as are encountered in an endeavour to breed a winner for coursing or racing. In coursing and racing, as I have already pointed out, there are other factors than good looks to be considered ; but in turning one's attention to the show ring good looks, as these are interpreted by the fraternity interested in that hobby, are paramount.

The one temperamental fault to beware of is that of shyness. Never breed from a shy or over nervy bitch. These faults will out and a bad shower is the abomination of abominations. No matter how beautiful your exhibit may be if he or she will not show good points go for nothing.

Having secured a bitch you need only see to it that she is in the best of health, and then at the proper age mate her to the champion dog which would appear to suit her best. Chose a dog not too nearly related, and one in which any weakness in the bitch can be counteracted by what in him is strong, but do not ever entertain the purchase of a bitch with a glaring weakness in the false hope that you can breed it out by choosing a dog with that fault entirely missing. Take, for instance, hereditary bad feet! A bitch with that bad fault will go on producing bad footed stock, no matter how good the feet of the dog may be. Thick heads are certain to come out again and again.

Do not think that by using a long headed dog of the orthodox type that you can counteract the bad head of the bitch. You cannot, and this I say most forcibly and definitely. Bad feet, *provided that they are not inherited,* may not be a serious drawback, but before purchasing a bitch with bad feet I would always like to be certain that in her youth, or, rather, at her birth, she possessed good feet of a perfect shape. Frequently bad rearing may permanently spoil a greyhound's feet, but in addition to the feet there is in that case almost certain to be something else amiss, such as weedy bone, flat sides or cowhocks.

To gain success, I would never breed from a bitch on her first heat. It is, however, a common custom amongst showmen to do so upon the ground that having a litter brings down the brisket and improves the bitch herself, but I would like to see one with a naturally deep brisket which has in no way been forced. At fourteen to sixteen months, therefore, which in the ordinary course will be the time of the bitche's second heat, mate her to the right dog and then give her every chance.

The feeding of the show bitch is of the greatest importance, especially for the formation of heads. She should never be loaded with food at one meal. She should be fed four times daily, the total weight of food being greater than her usual ration when not pregnant. If she be, say, sixty-eight pounds, her ordinary rations would be two pounds two ounces, but when pregnant this should be increased to two pounds and a half. Give three feeds during the day, of half a pound each, and the full pound for the last meal at night. It has been established beyond doubt that big meals constrict the heads of the developing pups.

Exercise should be of the free and easy kind. That is to say complete freedom from the time of mating right up to the end of the nine weeks ; taking care, of course, that the bitch has gone right off use before being turned loose. If she has been successfully mated, she would not run any risk even if mated by another dog, but if she were unsuccessfully mated it would be unpleasant to have a litter of mongrels. In any case your own common sense will advise you when she is safe.

I am a great believer in allowing bitches to do what they wish. They will look after themselves better than you can do it for them, and there is too much anxiety evinced upon the part of zealous owners when a bitch is in whelp. As to whelping, I have dealt with that subject earlier on in the book, so there will be no use in repeating myself, for the show greyhound, if somewhat different in many ways, is still a greyhound, and will whelp in the same way.

The management of the whelps up to weaning will be the same, but after that there are differences.

Practically all Cornish whelps are put out to walk. Many of them go to butchers, and, looking to the class of food they there obtain, it will be seen, if the book has been read thoroughly, that that will be conducive to the great size which is required in the show dog.

The butchers, cottagers and small farmers who in Cornwall take pups understand champion-making from start to finish. They know how to feed and how to handle. Everything (man and beast) is well fed in Cornwall. The pup gets the right food at home, and goodness knows how much he picks up during the day, and not offal at that.

" The Pasty " plays no small part in the raising of the Cornish dogs. The children go to school literally armed with pasties. Large, long, formidable looking pasties, with probably fish in one end, meat in the middle and cream and jam in the other end. A three course meal imprisoned in crust which is not always too light, but first class fare for a growing whelp. He does not take long to learn where the school is, and there he repairs daily at the dinner hour and does himself proud. He grows fat and grows sleek and that is what is required in growing a champion.

Then again, in the handling of the whelp is no small help in its development. From the day he arrives on his walk he is worshipped by the old man with a parent's pride. That the whelp is not his makes no difference. He gloats over him and fusses him and perches him on the table, putting one hand under his belly and gently raising him into a slight arch and this, repeated day by day, while the proud walker gazes with admiration, gradually trains the body into the desired shape, for the flat back is not the vogue on the show bench.

A famous breeder in Cornwall, who was also a great grower of rambler roses, said to me once, " I take the whelps every day from the time they are six weeks old and I bend them into shape just like the roses on the verandah which I train to go where I want them."

So it is, true every time. From earliest infancy the whelp learns what a collar is, he drags a lead about and this is picked up for a second at a time just to teach him what it is to be under restraint, but the process of actually breaking to the lead never takes place. It just comes.

When the whelp is a few weeks old, " Tommie," on coming home from school, is told to take " Fly " or " Spring " as the case may be—for every bitch is " Fly "

and every dog is "Spring" in Cornwall—just down
the road to the corner and back.

Fifty yards, perhaps, but it is all training ; and when
the budding champion attains to respectable size and
begins to show his great proportions, the governor
himself walks proudly out with his dog, the eyes of the
village upon him the while, admiring and commenting
on the likeness of the dog to Champion Tre Pol or
Pen-something-or-other that " won the best in show at
Cruft's just on twenty year ago."

There is no other part of England where walking is
done so thoroughly as in Cornwall, and envy that the dog
is somebody else's property never seems to detract from
the pride which is taken in the animal by the walker. I
stood one evening in the doorway of a village inn talking
to an old Cornish sportsman as a friend of his went past
with two really beautiful young greyhounds, and the
remark of my companion was typical: "If I
could walk down this 'ere street wi' two dogs like
they, I wouldn't call the King my uncle." It is a
mania, bred in the blood. Nothing is too good for
the puppies, and no time is begrudged in grooming
and hand rubbing and moulding them literally into
shape.

The youngsters never get long exercise, but they are
never left at home on the occasions when the master
visits the inn for a glass, or when he has to fetch his
'bacca. The lead is always in the pocket, and it is just

a case of a whistle and " Here, Fly, my darling," and on it goes and " Fly " has another airing, probably the twentieth that day.

In such hands there is no special process known as " Preparation for show." Many a Cornish dog is removed straight from his walk to the Agricultural Hall to sweep the boards and annex the championship. If it can be done that way, so much the better—but we do not all live in Cornwall. If, however, the method as I have tried to describe it can be carried out elsewhere, it will be unnecessary for me to go into technical details about preparation.

The greyhound is the show dog subject to the least faking. If you keep him well he will carry a coat which only requires grooming as an additional form of exercise. It beautifies itself, and the only tools necessary are a dandy, a hound-glove and a number six Spratt's metal comb.

Some dogs grow claws, in which case a nail cutter is necessary. Beyond the possible cutting back of the nails, the only other operation will be with reference to the tail, upon which, if any long or straggling hairs appear, these have to be removed. This is usually done with a little powdered resin put in the palm of the hand, then the tail taken gently through the hand from root to tip. The grip of the resined palm will remove all superfluous growth.

The handling of a greyhound in the ring is, however,

somewhat of a fine art and skilled job. A six feet lead
is usually employed, and your dog should be so trained
that he will walk freely without tightening the lead.
He should more or less walk by himself and obey the
slightest touch upon it. As many judges ask to see the
dog run he should have been trained to gallop nicely
in a space the size of the ring, which is not, as a rule, of
very ample proportions.

When being shown to the judge at rest, it is invariably
the rule that the handler will put his hand under the
flank and arch the dog, raising him on to his toes at
the same time. This is permissible, but it is a practice
which should not be encouraged.

The great Mr. Joseph Walker, for many years judge of
the Waterloo Cup, and one of the finest judges of a greyhound who has ever lived, was invited some years ago
to judge greyhounds at the Ladies' Kennel Association
Championship Show, and he said before entering the ring
that he would put down entirely every dog which was
thus interfered with, whether it were good, bad or
indifferent—and he did. He was never asked to judge
again.

Regarding registration, a show greyhound must be
registered at the Kennel Club. If the parents are
registered all that is necessary is to fill up the necessary
form and forward it with the fee of two shillings and
sixpence to the secretary of the club. If parents are
not registered, and no details as to breeding can be

procured, the dog can be certified by an expert as being a typical greyhound, and upon this any dog can be registered. Even if already registered in the G.S.B., a greyhound, if to be shown, must be registered with the Kennel Club.

## CHAPTER XXVII

### MY GREYHOUND AS A COMPANION

I CANNOT leave this engrossing subject without saying a word in praise of the most charming of dogs as a companion. In this capacity he has no rival. He is faithful, devoted, highly intelligent and all but human. His long and continued association with man makes him of necessity more human than other dogs, the oldest of which is young as compared with the greyhound in antiquity. He was, moreover, just as human nearly two thousand years ago, for the writer Arian has dealt in the most feeling manner possible with the companion side of the greyhound character, and what he had to say in his remote age is just exactly what those who know the greyhound are bound to write to-day.

The greyhound is essentially a sporting and utility dog, and, employed at his legitimate work, is probably where he is most happy; and far be it from me ever to keep a lot of idle greyhounds about me to make both them and myself unhappy—they by living in sloth, and myself by having to witness it—but one greyhound in my house is always the joy of joys.

It is a strange and wonderful fact that a greyhound which has never known what it is to live anywhere but in kennels, if introduced to the house, will settle there as it were by instinct and to the manner born. He is never from the first moment obtrusive or a nuisance; neither is he shy or awkward, but takes everything as it comes in the most natural way. One thing he must have, and this must be provided if he is going to be a house-dweller, and that is a comfortable and commodious easy chair. In this he will coil himself up and be happy for hours on end. He has an instinctive dislike of sleeping on the floor. He is a thin-skinned fellow and very subject to the unpleasant cold draughts from the bottoms of doors, so if not raised in a chair, is inclined to be just a tiny bit restless and will wander to and fro in search of a warm spot wherein to take his ease.

He loves attending at the dinner table. He stands patiently by, nosing one occasionally just to remind one that he is there and would like a choice morsel when convenient. His eyes the while would melt the stoniest of hearts, so much so that he may be spoiled by receiving too much attention at table, and it is always an injustice to spoil a dog in this way, for the time will come one day when you are not in the best of moods and when he will get on your nerves and then be banished from the room. When you next see him you will be consumed with remorse at the hurt expression in those liquid eyes. Those wistful, beseeching, pleading eyes brimming full of love will neither chide nor upbraid but will just say

more plainly than words: " Oh ! how you hurt me, and
what have I done to deserve it from you ? but let us be
friends and forget." Yes ! he does not only forgive,
he forgets too. If you have taken your greyhound to
your heart and made him one of the household,
treat him as such and he will not presume upon
you.

My greyhound in the house shall have a plate of
his own. Not a dog basin, but a dinner plate, and he
will eat what I eat and at the same time. This should
be the principle, whether it be in a castle or a cottage.
The greyhound is the daintiest of feeders, and can have
his plate on the costliest of carpets without any danger
of his making the slightest stain. He eats tastefully
and gracefully, with no unseemly sounds as do other dogs,
often to the annoyance of your guests.

As a walking companion the greyhound is the best
of all dogs. For miles he will walk by your side with
no need for the lead, and if he should ever make a
rush it will be after a rabbit ; this one is only too
prone to do oneself, and it is his nature more than ours.
In accompanying you on a ride where can you find a
better companion than the greyhound? He will walk,
trot, canter or gallop with like appreciation, and he loves
a horse as a sportsman loves a horse and is never
happier than when with one.

The greyhound is passionately devoted to young
children and would sacrifice his life in their defence,

and is pleased to spend his time amusing them in play the livelong day if called upon to do so.

As a guard the greyhound is marvellous. His sense of proprietorship, bred of his association with man throughout the ages, is greatly developed, and woe betide the unfortunate burglar who has to face the attack of an infuriated greyhound in defence of his master's property. He has; perhaps in an accentuated form beyond that of other dogs, a fine sense of discrimination as to who should and who should not enter the premises of his master. His intelligence defies all attempts at adequate description. There would appear to be nothing which he does not understand either in word or gesture or the shadow of coming events. When your favourite has done his work, cherish him and give him a place with yourself for the rest of his but too short life. It is his one drawback. He should live as long as his master.

THE END

# INDEX.

# INDEX

R

Printed in the United Kingdom
by Lightning Source UK Ltd.
109003UKS00001B/16